FILING Made EASY

A Filing Simulation

Fourth Edition

Ralph M. Holmes
Kathleen K. Conway

Glencoe McGraw-Hill

New York, New York   Columbus, Ohio   Woodland Hills, California   Peoria, Illinois

Reviewers

Glencoe/McGraw-Hill

A Division of The **McGraw·Hill** Companies

Filing Made Easy: A Filing Simulation, Fourth Edition
Imprint 2002

Components of the program:
Envelope Practice Set: 0-02-813831-7
Teacher Manual and Key: 0-02-813832-5

Send all inquiries to:
Glencoe/McGraw-Hill
21600 Oxnard Street, Suite 500
Woodland Hills, CA 91367

P/N G38317.23 of ISBN 0-02-813831-7

03 IPAK 10

Contents

Introduction 1

Unit 1   Alphabetic Card Filing 5

Unit 2   Alphabetic Correspondence Filing 42

Unit 3   Geographic Filing 59

Unit 4   Subject Filing 62

Unit 5   Numeric Filing 66

Unit 6   Filing Documents Electronically 69

Answers to Self-Check Exercises 73

Answers to Fast-Find Exercises 86

Proficiency Checkups 87

Practical Application Answer Sheets 95

Filing Checklist 107

Summary of Filing and Indexing Rules 109

State Abbreviations 112

Introduction

Did You Know That ....

According to one estimate, executives spend up to 6 weeks each year
searching for misfiled, misplaced, or mislabeled paperwork.

The success of any business depends to a large extent on how well it keeps
its records—letters, interoffice memorandums, invoices, reports, and so on.
Records are needed to ensure that the business operates smoothly, efficiently, and profitably. They are needed to record purchases and sales, handle
personnel matters, and respond to customer complaints. Records are the history of a company. They are the lifeblood of any business.

Records must be stored so that they are safe from damage or loss. They
must also be filed in such a way that they can be quickly and efficiently
retrieved when they are needed. Without a good storage and retrieval system for its records, a business or organization would find it very difficult to
operate efficiently.

Filing is the process of arranging and storing records in an orderly and
efficient manner so that records can be located quickly and efficiently.
Records may be filed in many ways, but the most common filing systems
are *alphabetic, geographic, subject,* and *numeric.* Many companies have con-
verted to electronic filing of records, but a knowledge of these four major
systems is still essential for a successful filing system.

In this simulation, you will learn the basic rules that apply to each of
the four most common filing systems used in business. These rules are based
on those established by the Association of Records Managers and
Administrators, Inc. (ARMA). As you learn the rules, you will practice filing
records in each of the four systems. With your knowledge of the most commonly accepted filing rules and basic filing systems, you should be able to
file materials in any business for which you might work.

Filing Fact

The Association of Records Managers and Administrators, Inc. (ARMA) is the international
organization for records managers. It has developed rules for indexing and alphabetizing
records. The rules presented in *Filing Made Easy* are based on those rules.

Interspersed throughout this student manual are special features titled
Filing Fact, On the Job, Technology in Filing, and *Task Tips.* Also included is a
problem-solving feature titled *"How Would You."* *Filing Fact, On the Job,
Technology in Filing,* and *Task Tips* provide facts and hints on the subject of
filing. Each *How Would You* feature presents a situation that requires you to
think about how you would resolve it. These features enlighten you and
offer you glimpses into the world of work.

Before You Begin

Before you start your work, check the materials in the large envelope to be
sure that you have everything you need. In addition to the book you are
now reading, you should have:

1. A pad of numbered cards (with miniature letters and cross-reference
   sheets printed on the back)

2. A fold-out file box
3. A set of six file guides marked A–B, C–D, E–F, G–H, I–J, and K–L
4. A set of six miniature file folders
5. A piece of cardboard

Report any missing items to your instructor at this time. Next, set up the file box as follows:

1. First, write your name in the proper space on the file box. Then, pull out the sides of the box so that it is square. (This is much like putting together a gift box from a department store.)
2. Remove the set of six file guides from the large envelope. Put the guides in the file box in alphabetical order: A–B, C–D, E–F, G–H, I–J, and K–L.
3. Remove the piece of cardboard from the envelope. You will see faint fold marks on one side. Fold the cardboard along the marks and put it behind the file guides. The piece of folded cardboard will ensure that the materials in the box stand up properly while you are filing.

Be sure to lay the materials flat in the file box and close the lid at the end of each class period so the cards and letters you are working with will not be disturbed. Store any other materials you are not using in the large envelope.

Now you are ready to begin your work.

Welcome to Reade & Relaxe Book Centers

Did You Know That ....
Today, workers change jobs at least seven times during their work lives.

You have been employed as a summer intern records management associate at the corporate offices of Reade & Relaxe Book Centers in Minneapolis, Minnesota. This is a relatively new company that has been in operation only 10 years. There are Reade & Relaxe Book Centers in 35 cities throughout the nation, and the number of Centers is growing rapidly.

Reade & Relaxe Book Centers are large bookstores that offer a relaxed and inviting environment in which to purchase books and music. Each Center has a large stock of books covering many subjects. There are children's books, fiction and nonfiction books, reference books, and so on. The Center also sells CDs, cassette tapes, and videos to suit a wide variety of musical tastes.

Customers can browse among the books, listen to music before making their selection, or examine books and magazines in quiet corners. There is a special children's area in each Center with books, games, and a story-telling corner. There is even a coffee shop in one section of the Center where customers can meet, talk about books, or listen to live music in the evenings while enjoying gourmet snacks and beverages. The Centers are rapidly becoming popular community meeting places.

The corporate office is responsible for coordinating all activities of the stores throughout the country. A large office staff maintains sales, purchases, advertising, and personnel records. The staff also designs special campaigns, handles author relations, manages sales and purchases, and selects locations for new store sites.

Key People at Reade & Relaxe Book Centers

In your work as a summer intern records management associate, you will have an opportunity to meet many of the people who work at the corporate headquarters of Reade & Relaxe Book Centers. As you complete the training program, you will be working with the records of four of the executives in the corporate offices.

Maria Sanchez, Chief Executive Officer

Maria Sanchez was one of the founders of Reade & Relaxe Book Centers. A Minneapolis native, Maria had previously worked for a large local bookstore, starting as a summer intern while she was a college student. Her belief that bookstores should be friendly, comfortable places led to the founding of Reade & Relaxe. Maria's interest in literacy and environmental issues have resulted in corporate initiatives.

Jeffrey Silverstein, Promotions Director

Jeffrey Silverstein has known Maria Sanchez for over 20 years and was an initial investor in the company. Just a year after the company was formed, Maria was able to lure Jeffrey from his advertising position in Chicago. He enjoys the simpler lifestyle of the Twin Cities area and has been able to hone his snow-skiing skills in his spare time.

Montigo Washington, Distribution Services Director

Montigo had worked with Maria Sanchez earlier but joined Reade & Relaxe Book Centers only about 5 years ago, shortly after the company began its tremendous growth. Her computer skills and understanding of the book-sellers' industry have smoothed the way for the opening of numerous stores across the country. When she is not traveling to potential store sites, Montigo and her husband raise AKC beagles.

Linda Richards, Human Resources Director

Linda Richards has been with Reade & Relaxe Book Centers since its founding. She began working part-time in the Human Resources Department while she attended college. After she earned her master's degree two years ago, she was promoted to Human Resources Director. Linda has two young children, and it was at her urging that the company started its Saturday morning children's reading sessions.

Filing Fact

File clerks and other office workers are not the only people who need an understanding of basic filing rules. Everyone has files of some sort—income tax records, canceled checks, bills paid and unpaid, recipes, medical records. Without some sort of filing system, finding one item among all of your records would be time-consuming and perhaps frustrating.

The Training Program

When you applied for the job as a records management associate, you told Linda Richards that you did not know how to file but were willing to learn. Ms. Richards said that Reade & Relaxe has an excellent on-the-job training program that will teach you how to file. As you learn, you will be working with the records of the company.

The training program at Reade & Relaxe Book Centers will teach you how to file using their filing systems. The program will help you learn the filing rules well before you are tested on your understanding. After each filing rule is presented in an easy-to-understand manner, you will study an example of how the rule actually works. Next, you will complete a *self-check exercise* to practice that rule. In each self-check exercise, you will check your own work. You will not be penalized for any mistakes; however, it is very important that you understand why you made a mistake before you correct it. In this way, you can be sure that you understand each rule before you go to the next one.

After you are satisfied that you clearly understand a block of five rules, you will complete a *self-check review exercise* and, if necessary, a *self-check reinforcement exercise.* Then you will complete a *proficiency checkup,* which will be graded by your supervisor (your instructor). *Practical applications* and *fast-find exercises* will give you joblike experience in using the rules; you will file cards and letters under the direction of the filing supervisor. There will even be opportunities for extra practice if you need it or if it is suggested by your supervisor.

When you have successfully completed the Reade & Relaxe Centers' training program, you will receive a certificate of proficiency. You will then begin your work as a records management associate with the company.

You are now ready to start your training program. Turn to Unit 1 on the next page and begin.

ON THE JOB

Manual dexterity, good eyesight, and a good memory are important skills for file clerks. They classify, store, retrieve, and update office information on request; examine incoming mail and code it; store documents; film documents for storage on microforms or optical disks; and check files at regular intervals.

Alphabetic Card Filing

After you have completed this unit, you will be able to

- Define *filing,* and explain how indexing facilitates the filing process.
- Index personal and business names in correct filing order.
- Arrange address cards in correct alphabetical order.
- Retrieve specific address cards filed in alphabetical order.

Filing Fact

A *card file* is easy to maintain, is easy to file, and is easy to retrieve data from.

In this unit you will learn the basic rules for filing personal and business names. You will also practice filing address cards in an alphabetic system. Before you start, familiarize yourself with the following basic terms.

Filing is the process of arranging and storing records in an orderly and consistent manner and in a safe place so that the records can be located and used quickly and easily.

Filing units are the parts of a name used to determine the order in which the name will be filed.

Filing segments are one or more filing units, such as the entire name or a part of the name, which are used for filing purposes.

Indexing is the process of arranging the filing units of a name to place the name in correct filing order.

Alphabetizing is the process of placing names in order according to the letters of the alphabet.

Indexing

Before names of individuals can be alphabetized (placed in alphabetical order), they must be *indexed* (rearranged) into filing units. The filing units can then be used to decide alphabetical order.

Personal names are indexed into units in the following order: (1) last name (surname), (2) first name or initial, and (3) middle name or initial (if any). For example, the name *Chris Lynn Davis* is indexed into units as:

Unit 1	Unit 2	Unit 3
Davis	Chris	Lynn

Punctuation marks, including periods, commas, dashes, hyphens, apostrophes, and so on, are ignored when indexing. For example, the name *Florence R. Abrams* is indexed as:

Unit 1	Unit 2	Unit 3
Abrams	Florence	R

The name *F. N. Sanchez* is indexed as:

Unit 1	Unit 2	Unit 3
Sanchez	F	N

Technology in Filing

On a computer database, an indexing unit is called a "field."

Technology in Filing

Within word processing programs, placing information in some kind of order, such as alphabetic or numeric, is often called *sorting*.

A name with only two parts—a last name and a first name—has only two units. The name *Marie Smith* is indexed as:

Unit 1
Smith

Unit 2
Marie

Study the following examples to see how other names are indexed. As you see, the last name (surname) is the first unit. The first name or initial is the second unit. The middle name or initial is the third unit. Notice too that punctuation marks are ignored in indexing.

Names	Unit 1	Unit 2	Unit 3
Mary Ann Bates	Bates	Mary	Ann
John D. Crocker	Crocker	John	D
D. Q. Franco	Franco	D	Q
Matthew Riggins	Riggins	Matthew	

Now see if you can index the following names by writing the units for each name in the proper spaces. In all exercises, use a pencil so you can easily erase and correct your errors. (Remember to ignore punctuation marks.)

Names	Unit 1	Unit 2	Unit 3
1. Faye Lee Anderson			
2. D. J. Barnes			
3. Shannon T. Grace			
4. Thomas Roy Harris			
5. Arturo Rodriquez			

Did you get the following answers?

	Unit 1	Unit 2	Unit 3
1.	Anderson	Faye	Lee
2.	Barnes	D	J
3.	Grace	Shannon	T
4.	Harris	Thomas	Roy
5.	Rodriquez	Arturo	

Make any corrections that are needed. Then index the following names.

Names	Unit 1	Unit 2	Unit 3
1. Lucy O. Adams			
2. Arthur David Chung			
3. Della Ann Jacobs			
4. Daniel Kingston			
5. A. Donald Traxler			

Did you get the following answers?

	Unit 1	Unit 2	Unit 3
1.	Adams	Lucy	O
2.	Chung	Arthur	David
3.	Jacobs	Della	Ann
4.	Kingston	Daniel	
5.	Traxler	A	Donald

Now that you have had some practice in indexing, you are ready to begin your study of filing rules.

Filing Fact

"Records management" refers to the procedures established to file, maintain, and retrieve records. The filing rules you will learn in this simulation are just one aspect of records management.

SECTION ONE • Rules 1-5

Study the following rules and examples, and complete the self-check exercise for each rule. Check your answers against those given in the self-check answer section, which begins on page 73. If you make any errors in these exercises, review the appropriate rule and correct your errors. Be sure that you understand each rule *thoroughly* before going to a new rule.

RULE 1 • Alphabetizing Names

After names have been indexed, they can be alphabetized (placed in correct alphabetical order) by comparing them unit by unit and letter by letter as follows:

1. Compare the *first units* of the names letter by letter.
2. If the first units are identical, compare the *second units* letter by letter.
3. If the first two units are identical, compare the *third units* letter by letter, and so on.

Remember to index *all* the names in the exercise *before* you place them in alphabetical order. Remove all punctuation marks as you index and alphabetize each name. In the examples below, the letter that determines the alphabetical order has been underlined.

	Names	Unit 1	Unit 2	Unit 3		ALPHABETICAL ORDER
1.	Lenny Williams	Williams	Lenny			Clanton Anthony Ray
2.	Dan O. Winton	Winton	Dan	O		Clanton Anthony Roy
3.	Anthony Roy Clanton	Clanton	Anthony	Roy		Clarkston Raye
4.	Anthony Ray Clanton	Clanton	Anthony	Ray		Williams Lenny
5.	Raye Clarkston	Clarkston	Raye			Winton Dan O

 **SELF-CHECK • Exercise 1a**

Index the following names in the first three columns. Then place the names in alphabetical order in the last column.

Names	Unit 1	Unit 2	Unit 3	ALPHABETICAL ORDER
1. Jane Alice Grimm				
2. Jane Ann Grimm				
3. Richard R. Gilley				
4. Faith Ann Grayson				
5. Richard T. Gilley				

After completing the exercise, check your answers against those in the answer section that begins on page 73. Whenever you are instructed to check your answers, refer to this answer section.

 **SELF-CHECK • Exercise 1b**

Index and alphabetize the following names in the spaces provided.

Names	Unit 1	Unit 2	Unit 3	ALPHABETICAL ORDER
1. Raoul Massey				
2. Ralph Massey				
3. Rolly A. Massey				
4. Arturo A. Quiroga				
5. Arthur X. Quirroga				

Check your answers.

RULE 2 • Nicknames and Abbreviated First Names

Nicknames of individuals (such as *Jimmy, Annie,* and *Johnny*) are indexed and alphabetized as written—in the same way that other first names are indexed and alphabetized as written.

Abbreviated first names of individuals (such as *Wm., Robt.,* and *Chas.*) are indexed and alphabetized as they are written in *abbreviated form*. Abbreviated names are *not* spelled out. Also remember that punctuation marks are ignored when names are indexed and alphabetized.

Names	Unit 1	Unit 2	Unit 3	ALPHABETICAL ORDER
1. Ricky Alton	Alton	Ricky		Adams Wm
2. Susie Marie Amos	Amos	Susie	Marie	Addis Chas Henry
3. Robt. Addison	Addison	Robt		Addison Robt
4. Chas. Henry Addis	Addis	Chas	Henry	Alton Ricky
5. Wm. Adams	Adams	Wm		Amos Susie Marie

 **SELF-CHECK • Exercise 2**

Index and alphabetize the following names in the spaces provided.

Names	Unit 1	Unit 2	Unit 3	ALPHABETICAL ORDER
1. Charro Hay	_____	_____	_____	_____
2. Teddy Hayes	_____	_____	_____	_____
3. Chas. Ray Hay	_____	_____	_____	_____
4. Thos. Hayes	_____	_____	_____	_____
5. Susie Hanes	_____	_____	_____	_____

Check your answers.

RULE 3 • Nothing Before Something

A single-unit name (a name that has only one indexing unit) such as *Zack* or *Smith* is alphabetized *before* the same name that has additional filing units. For example, the name *Zack* is alphabetized before the name *James Zack.*

A last name with a first initial only is alphabetized before the same last name that has a full first name beginning with the same letter. For example, the name *B. Thomas* is alphabetized before the name *Betty Thomas.*

In other words, **nothing comes before something** when placing names in correct alphabetical order.

Names	Unit 1	Unit 2	Unit 3	ALPHABETICAL ORDER
1. Mayer Thom	Thom	Mayer		Thom
2. M. Thompson	Thompson	M		Thom Mayer
3. Matthew Thompson	Thompson	Matthew		Thomas Mayer
4. Mayer T. Thomas	Thomas	Mayer	T	Thomas Mayer T
5. Mayer Thomas	Thomas	Mayer		Thompson M
6. Thom	Thom			Thompson Matthew

✔ SELF-CHECK • Exercise 3

Index and alphabetize the following names in the spaces provided.

	Names	Unit 1	Unit 2	Unit 3	ALPHABETICAL ORDER
1.	Mannie Franko				
2.	M. Franko				
3.	David T. Orville				
4.	Orville				
5.	D. Orville				

Check your answers.

> ### Filing Fact
> A *prefix* is a letter or letters that are placed in front of a word or name. Prefixes in personal names are not usually hyphenated.

RULE 4 • Names with Prefixes

A last name that begins with a *prefix* (such as *Mc*Lean or *De* Leon) is considered to be one unit even if there is a space between the prefix and the rest of the name. In indexing and alphabetizing, the prefix and the last name are written as one word with no spaces or punctuation marks.

Some common prefixes are *d', D', Da, de, De, Del, De la, Della, Den, Des, Di, Du, El, Fitz, L', La, Las, Le, Les, Lo, Los, M', Mac, Mc, O', Saint, San, St., Ste., Te, Ten, Ter, Van, Van de, Van der, Von,* and *Von der.* When indexing and alphabetizing, do not spell out the prefixes *St.* and *Ste.* (for *Saint*). Index and file them as written.

	Names	Unit 1	Unit 2	Unit 3	ALPHABETICAL ORDER
1.	Marcus T. McDonald	McDonald	Marcus	T	DelRio Marie
2.	Marie Del Rio	DelRio	Marie		DeRicco John
3.	Manny San August	SanAugust	Manny		McDonald Marcus T
4.	Mary St. Augustine	StAugustine	Mary		SanAugust Manny
5.	John De Ricco	DeRicco	John		StAugustine Mary

✔ SELF-CHECK • Exercise 4

Index and alphabetize the following names in the spaces provided.

	Names	Unit 1	Unit 2	Unit 3	ALPHABETICAL ORDER
1.	Andrew A. LaDona	_____	_____	_____	_____
2.	Martha F. St. Iverson	_____	_____	_____	_____
3.	Ann LaSalle	_____	_____	_____	_____
4.	Ruth Ann O'Donald	_____	_____	_____	_____
5.	Randolph A. O'Donnell	_____	_____	_____	_____

Check your answers.

RULE 5 • Hyphenated Names

Hyphenated names (such as *Anne-Marie* or *Kubelek-Levine*) are considered to be one unit. In indexing and alphabetizing, ignore the hyphen and write the two words together as one unit.

	Names	Unit 1	Unit 2	Unit 3	ALPHABETICAL ORDER
1.	Lisa J. Mayer-Archer	MayerArcher	Lisa	J	Martine JohnPaul
2.	Mark Simpson-Rye	SimpsonRye	Mark		MayerArcher Lisa J
3.	Jennifer Sipes-Ryan	SipesRyan	Jennifer		RobinArcher Maria C
4.	John-Paul Martine	Martine	JohnPaul		SimpsonRye Mark
5.	Maria C. Robin-Archer	RobinArcher	Maria	C	SipesRyan Jennifer

✔ SELF-CHECK • Exercise 5

Index and alphabetize the following names in the spaces provided.

	Names	Unit 1	Unit 2	Unit 3	ALPHABETICAL ORDER
1.	Lon Brace-Marcus	_____	_____	_____	_____
2.	Fred Brace-Mason	_____	_____	_____	_____
3.	Mark-Brent Silas	_____	_____	_____	_____
4.	Lon Brent Marcos	_____	_____	_____	_____
5.	Frederick Brade-Milkins	_____	_____	_____	_____

Check your answers.

 **SELF-CHECK • Review Exercise 1**

The following exercise is based on filing rules 1–5. Index and alphabetize the following names in the spaces provided.

	Names	Unit 1	Unit 2	Unit 3	ALPHABETICAL ORDER
1.	Sharon Jean Breen				
2.	S. T. Breene				
3.	Jason St. Rafter				
4.	Breen				
5.	Joan Sans-Rafter				
6.	Lonnie d'Aquisto				
7.	Susie de Royal				
8.	Geo. San Michaels				
9.	S. Breene				
10.	W. Breene Rafter				

Check your answers.

If you had any errors in indexing or alphabetizing, refer to the rule column alongside the name in the answer section. Review the rule and make needed corrections in your answers. Be sure you understand *all* the rules.

If you made any mistakes at all, complete Self-Check Reinforcement Exercise 1, which follows.

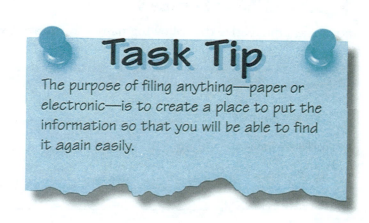

Task Tip

The purpose of filing anything—paper or electronic—is to create a place to put the information so that you will be able to find it again easily.

✓ SELF-CHECK • Reinforcement Exercise 1

The following exercise is based on filing rules 1–5. Index and alphabetize the names in the spaces provided.

Names	Unit 1	Unit 2	Unit 3	ALPHABETICAL ORDER
1. Wilma-Jean Braun				
2. Maxine el Dorado				
3. Jonathon Ste. Lorraine				
4. Braun				
5. Chas. St. Laurence				
6. S. Braune				
7. M. Brauning				
8. S. Braune Dawkins				
9. Michael Sans-Laurence				
10. A. B. Brauning				

Check your answers.

If you are sure you have mastered the first five rules, remove Proficiency Checkup 1 from page 87. Complete the checkup and submit it to your supervisor for evaluation. Then, with the approval of your supervisor, complete Practical Application 1 and Fast-Find Exercise 1, which follow.

PRACTICAL APPLICATION 1

1. From the pad of cards in the envelope, remove the cards numbered 1–20. (The numbers are in the upper right corner of each card.) Ignore the business letters on the back. They will be used in future activities.
2. The names on the cards already appear in correct indexing order. It is your task to arrange the cards in alphabetical order. To do this efficiently, sort the cards into piles—one pile for each letter of the alphabet. In each pile, arrange the cards in alphabetical order. Then combine the piles into one pile so that all the cards are in alphabetical order.

3. Remove the answer sheet for Practical Application 1 from the back of this manual (see page 95). List the numbers of the cards in the order in which you have arranged them. The numbers of the first three cards should be 14, 4, and 2.
4. Finally, place the cards *behind* the proper guides in the file box. For example, card 14 would be placed behind the C–D guide.
5. Submit the answer sheet to your supervisor. *Leave the cards in the box.*

FAST-FIND • Exercise 1

To be able to file materials accurately and quickly is important; however, you must also be able to find (retrieve) the materials just as accurately and quickly. The fast-find exercises will give you an opportunity to demonstrate how well you know indexing and alphabetizing rules and how quickly you can find filed materials.

Follow these steps for all fast-find exercises.

1. Record your *Beginning Time* in the blank.
2. Locate as rapidly as you can the listed names, using all the cards in the file box. As you locate each card in the file, record its number on the line to the right of the name.
3. As soon as you finish, record your *Ending Time*.
4. Subtract your beginning time from your ending time. Record this as your *Completion Time*.
5. Check your answers against those on page 86 in the back of this manual. Record the number of errors you made. For each incorrect answer, add 30 seconds to your completion time as a penalty. Record your *Penalty Time*.
6. Add your penalty time to the completion time to get your *Total Time*.
7. If time permits. Repeat the exercise. Try to lower your total time by at least 30 seconds.

Names to Be Located	*Number*	*Time*	
1. Betty Elaine Carel-Grande	_____	Ending Time	_____
2. M. D. De Lama	_____	− Beginning Time	_____
3. Windella Hillis-Audson	_____	Completion Time	_____
4. Ralph Ray Carel	_____	+ Penalty Time	_____
5. R. J. FitzGerald	_____	Total Time	_____
6. Mildred Chann	_____		
7. Rachael Ignasteo	_____	Errors	_____
8. Marty Damonde	_____		
9. Larry Chang	_____		
10. M. U. Hillis	_____		

Suppose you were going to keep in a file drawer a folder for each of your classes. Would you arrange the folders in alphabetical order or in the sequence that the classes occur during the day? Which way do you think would be more helpful? If you arranged the folders alphabetically, how would you identify the folders—generically by topic (math, science, social studies) or specifically by course name (Pre-Algebra, Chemistry, American History)?

Now suppose you were also labeling the dividers in your notebook. Would you arrange the notebook dividers in alphabetical order or in the sequence that the classes occur during the day? Which way do you think would be more helpful? How would you label the dividers?

With the approval of your supervisor, begin work on Section Two.

SECTION TWO • Rules 6-10

Study the following rules and examples. Complete the self-check exercise for each rule. Check your answers against those given in the self-check answer section, which begins on page 73. If you make any errors in these exercises, review the rule and correct your errors. *Be sure that you understand each rule thoroughly before going to a new rule.*

RULE 6 • Unusual and Foreign Names

When it is hard to determine which part of an unusual or foreign name is the surname (last name), consider the last written part to be the surname.

	Names	Unit 1	Unit 2	Unit 3	ALPHABETICAL ORDER
1.	Tre Neu Than	Than	Tre	Neu	Kelly Kipperson
2.	Thatcher W. Thorne	Thorne	Thatcher	W	Kesseck Heddy
3.	Kipperson Kelly	Kelly	Kipperson		Kwan Ho Quan
4.	Heddy Kesseck	Kesseck	Heddy		Than Tre Neu
5.	Ho Quan Kwan	Kwan	Ho	Quan	Thorne Thatcher W

✔ SELF-CHECK • Exercise 6

Index and alphabetize the following names in the spaces provided.

	Names	Unit 1	Unit 2	Unit 3	ALPHABETICAL ORDER
1.	Fairly Right				
2.	Olna Faith Right				
3.	Mew Leu Riew				
4.	Ramond Frank				
5.	Franco Ramondo				

Check your answers.

RULE 7 • Seniority Designations

When identical names have seniority designations (such as *3rd, II, Jr.,* and *Sr.*), the seniority designations become the last indexing unit and are used to determine the correct alphabetical order.

Arabic numbers (such as *3rd* and *4th*) are filed *before* all Roman numerals (such as *III* and *IV*). Both Arabic and Roman numbers are filed in numeric order before the words *Jr.* and *Sr.*

	Names	Unit 1	Unit 2	Unit 3	Unit 4	ALPHABETICAL ORDER
1.	J. T. Black, Sr.	Black	J	T	Sr	Black J T Jr
2.	Henry O. Blackmon, III	Blackmon	Henry	O	III	Black J T Sr
3.	Henry O. Blackmon, 4th	Blackmon	Henry	O	4th	Blackmon Henry O 4th
4.	J. T. Black, Jr.	Black	J	T	Jr	Blackmon Henry O II
5.	Henry O. Blackmon, II	Blackmon	Henry	O	II	Blackmon Henry O III

 SELF-CHECK • Exercise 7

Index and alphabetize the following names in the spaces provided.

	Names	Unit 1	Unit 2	Unit 3	Unit 4	ALPHABETICAL ORDER
1.	B. T. Jones, III					
2.	B. T. Jones, 4th					
3.	Brett T. Jonas, Jr.					
4.	B. T. Jones, II					
5.	Brett T. Jonas, Sr.					

Check your answers.

RULE 8 • Titles and Degrees

Professional titles (such as *Dr., Mayor, Senator*), personal titles (such as *Mr., Mrs., Ms.*), military ranks (such as *Major, Gen., Private*), and academic degrees (such as *Ph.D., M.A., M.D.*) are not considered in filing except to distinguish between two or more identical names. They are considered the last indexing unit (after all other units, including seniority titles).

	Names	Unit 1	Unit 2	Unit 3	ALPHABETICAL ORDER
1.	Mayor May Braxe	Braxe	May	Mayor	Braxe Brad Dr
2.	Brad Braxe, M.D.	Braxe	Brad	MD	Braxe Brad MD
3.	Mrs. May Braxe	Braxe	May	Mrs	Braxe May Mayor
4.	Dr. Brad Braxe	Braxe	Brad	Dr	Braxe May Mrs
5.	General Brax Marlow	Marlow	Brax	General	Marlow Brax General

✔ **SELF-CHECK • Exercise 8**

Index and alphabetize the following names in the spaces provided.

Names	Unit 1	Unit 2	Unit 3	ALPHABETICAL ORDER
1. Mr. Martin Angelo				
2. Mrs. Judie Angelo				
3. Major Angelo Martin				
4. Dr. Martin Angelo				
5. Angelo Martin, Ph.D.				

Check your answers.

RULE 9 • Religious and Royal Titles and Pseudonyms

Personal names that begin with religious or royal titles (such as *Father* or *Queen*) followed by only a first name are indexed and alphabetized as written. A pseudonym (a made-up name, such as *Little Richard*) is indexed and alphabetized as written.

Names	Unit 1	Unit 2	ALPHABETICAL ORDER
1. Father Lawrence	Father	Lawrence	Fathe Larry
2. Princess Lillian	Princess	Lillian	Father Lawrence
3. Mr. Clean	Mr	Clean	Mr Clean
4. Professor Lookalike	Professor	Lookalike	Princess Lillian
5. Larry Fathe	Fathe	Larry	Professor Lookalike

✔ **SELF-CHECK • Exercise 9**

Index and alphabetize the following names in the spaces provided.

Names	Unit 1	Unit 2	ALPHABETICAL ORDER
1. Queen Victoria			
2. Victor Brothers			
3. Prof. Analytical			
4. Sister Anna			
5. Brother Victor			

Check your answers.

When two or more names are identical, the addresses are used to determine the correct filing order. The parts of the address are compared in the following order: (1) town or city name, (2) state or province name, (3) street name, and (4) house or building number in ascending numeric order.

	Names	Unit 1	Unit 2	Unit 3	Unit 4	Unit 5	Unit 6
1.	Patrice Sanchez 116 Center Street Jackson, Georgia	Sanchez	Patrice	Jackson	Georgia	Center Street	116
2.	Patrice Sanchez 116 Center Street Jackson, Ohio	Sanchez	Patrice	Jackson	Ohio	Center Street	116
3.	Patrice Sanchez 1480 Blake Street Jackson, Ohio	Sanchez	Patrice	Jackson	Ohio	Blake Street	1480
4.	Patrice Sanchez 228 Center Street Jackson, Georgia	Sanchez	Patrice	Jackson	Georgia	Center Street	228
5.	Patrice Sanchez 116 Center Street Cincinnati, Ohio	Sanchez	Patrice	Cincinnati	Ohio	Center Street	116

ALPHABETICAL ORDER

Sanchez Patrice Cincinnati Ohio 116 Center Street

Sanchez Patrice Jackson Georgia 116 Center Street

Sanchez Patrice Jackson Georgia 228 Center Street

Sanchez Patrice Jackson Ohio 1480 Blake Street

Sanchez Patrice Jackson Ohio 116 Center Street

Task Tip

It is not necessarily a compliment to be known as the only person who can find something in your files.

 **SELF-CHECK • Exercise 10**

Index and alphabetize the following names in the spaces provided.

Names	Unit 1	Unit 2	Unit 3	Unit 4	Unit 5	Unit 6
1. Lamar Jefferson 228 Landmark Place Bradley, Indiana	_____	_____	_____	_____	_____	_____
2. Lamar Jefferson 2820 Landmark Street Bradley, Iowa	_____	_____	_____	_____	_____	_____
3. Lamar Jefferson 1630 Landmark Street Bradley, Iowa	_____	_____	_____	_____	_____	_____
4. Lamar Jefferson 486 Long Circle Bradley, Illinois	_____	_____	_____	_____	_____	_____
5. Lamar Jefferson 1500 Zenith Street Bradley, Iowa	_____	_____	_____	_____	_____	_____

ALPHABETICAL ORDER

_____

_____

_____

_____

_____

Check your answers.

The following exercise is based on filing rules 6–10. Index and alphabetize the following names in the spaces provided.

Names	Unit 1	Unit 2	Unit 3	Unit 4	Unit 5	Unit 6
1. Lela Biles 201 Zephyr Street Columbus, Ohio	___	___	___	___	___	___
2. Duchess Beatrice	___	___	___	___	___	___
3. Ronald Billey, Jr.	___	___	___	___	___	___
4. Lela Biles 221 Zephyr Street Columbus, Ohio	___	___	___	___	___	___
5. Leland Biles, Ph.D.	___	___	___	___	___	___
6. Ronald Billey, 3rd	___	___	___	___	___	___
7. Doctor Fixit	___	___	___	___	___	___
8. Ronald Billey, Sr.	___	___	___	___	___	___
9. Dr. Leland Biles	___	___	___	___	___	___
10. Reyno Bilaufa	___	___	___	___	___	___

ALPHABETICAL ORDER

_____

_____

_____

_____

_____

_____

_____

_____

_____

_____

Check your answers.

If you had any errors in indexing or alphabetizing, review the rule listed alongside the name in the answer section. Make needed corrections in your answers. Be sure that you understand *all* the rules.

If you made any mistakes at all, complete Self-Check Reinforcement Exercise 2, which follows.

✔ SELF-CHECK • Reinforcement Exercise 2

The following exercise is based on filing rules 6–10. Index and alphabetize the following names in the spaces provided.

	Names	Unit 1	Unit 2	Unit 3	Unit 4	Unit 5	Unit 6
1.	James Kingsley 600 Center Street Orlando, Florida						
2.	King James						
3.	Jadeth King, Jr.						
4.	James Kingsley 460 Peak Street Orlando, Florida						
5.	Kingston James, M.D.						
6.	Jadeth King, 3rd						
7.	Jamal Sheik						
8.	Jadeth King, Sr.						
9.	Kingston James, Ph.D.						
10.	Mrs. James King						

ALPHABETICAL ORDER

_____

_____

_____

_____

_____

_____

_____

_____

_____

_____

Check your answers.

If you are sure you have mastered the first ten rules, remove Proficiency Checkup 2 from page 89. Complete the checkup and submit it to your supervisor for evaluation. Then, with the approval of your supervisor, complete Practical Applications 2 and 3 and Fast-Find Exercise 2, which follow.

PRACTICAL APPLICATION 2

1. From the pad of cards, remove the cards numbered 21–40. The numbers are in the upper right corner of each card. (Ignore the business letters on the back. They will be used in future activities.)
2. The names on the cards are already in correct indexing order. Now, arrange the cards in alphabetical order. To do this efficiently, sort the cards into piles—one pile for each letter of the alphabet. Then arrange the cards in each pile in alphabetical order. Finally, place all the cards in alphabetical order. *Do not put the cards in the file box.*
3. Remove the answer sheet for Practical Application 2 from the back of this manual. List the numbers of the cards in the order in which you have arranged them.
4. Submit the answer sheet to your supervisor. Clip the cards together and place them in the large envelope until you are ready to complete Practical Application 3.

PRACTICAL APPLICATION 3

1. From the large envelope, remove the cards you used in Practical Application 2.
2. File the cards in alphabetical order in the file box with the other cards.
3. Remove the answer sheet for Practical Application 3 from the back of this manual. List the numbers of *all* the cards in the file box in the order in which you have filed them.
4. Submit the answer sheet to your supervisor. *Leave the cards in the box.*

FAST-FIND • Exercise 2

Complete this exercise following the instructions for Fast-Find Exercise 1 on page 14.

	Names to Be Located	Number		Time
1.	H. W. Jackstone, 3rd	_____	Ending Time	_____
2.	Alma Hinson Hewett, M.A.	_____	− Beginning Time	_____
3.	Marrianne L. Fluger	_____	Completion Time	_____
4.	Brother Alexander	_____	+ Penalty Time	_____
5.	Dr. Joanne E. Fath	_____	Total Time	_____
6.	Alana O. Heye	_____		
7.	H. W. Jackstone, Jr.	_____	Errors	_____
8.	King George	_____		
9.	Leu Vi Heye	_____		
10.	Geraldine R. Fitz	_____		

You just got a new address book and are excited about putting your friends' names in it. Under which letter would you place these names: Terry O'Connor, Gina Griffin-Amcor, Dan Van Camp, Wo Zhen, Tony de Felice, Grant Andrew?

With the approval of your supervisor, begin work on Section Three.

SECTION THREE • Rules 11–15

Study the following rules and examples. Complete the self-check exercise for each rule. Then check your answers with those given in the self-check answer section, which begins on page 73. If you make any errors in these exercises, review the rule and correct your errors. Be sure that you understand each rule thoroughly before going to a new rule.

RULE 11 • Company Names

Company and organization names are indexed and alphabetized as written. Personal names that appear in company names are indexed and filed *as written;* they are *not* transposed (rearranged).

Prepositions (such as *in, of, at*), conjunctions (such as *and, but, or*), and articles (such as *a, an*) in company names are considered to be separate filing units. However, when *The* is the first word of the company name, it is indexed and filed as the *last* unit.

	Names	Unit 1	Unit 2	Unit 3	Unit 4	Unit 5
1.	Rose T. Aaronsen Books	Rose	T	Aaronsen	Books	
2.	Aaron Quick Book Store	Aaron	Quick	Book	Store	
3.	The Quaint and Quiet Shoppe	Quaint	and	Quiet	Shoppe	The
4.	Quick Action Data Retrieval	Quick	Action	Data	Retrieval	
5.	Axel Queen Magazines	Axel	Queen	Magazines		

ALPHABETICAL ORDER

A̲aron Quick Book Store

A̲xel Queen Magazines

Q̲uaint and Quiet Shoppe The

Q̲uick Action Data Retrieval

R̲ose T Aaronsen Books

Index and alphabetize the following names in the spaces provided.

Names	Unit 1	Unit 2	Unit 3	Unit 4
1. Bean Pot Company				
2. Ann Byers Music Company				
3. The Amplifier Works				
4. A. Aggasi Sports Company				
5. Andrews Machines, Incorporated				

ALPHABETICAL ORDER

_____

_____

_____

_____

_____

Check your answers.

RULE 12 • Abbreviations and Single Letters in Company Names

Abbreviations in a company name (such as *Mfg., Inc,* and *Co.*) are indexed and alphabetized as written, omitting punctuation marks.

If a company name contains single letters with spaces between the letters (such as *A B C Company*), each letter is a separate indexing unit. If there are no spaces between the letters (such as in *CU Finance Company*), all of the letters are indexed and alphabetized as *one* unit.

Names	Unit 1	Unit 2	Unit 3	Unit 4		ALPHABETICAL ORDER
1. A B C Travel	A	B	C	Travel		<u>A</u> B C Travel
2. Alton Research Group	Alton	Research	Group			<u>AA</u> Bookbinders
3. AA Bookbinders	AA	Bookbinders				<u>Al</u>ton Research Group
4. BBB Books	BBB	Books				<u>Ba</u>ron Printing Co
5. Baron Printing Co.	Baron	Printing	Co			<u>BB</u>B Books

Index and alphabetize the following names in the spaces provided.

	Names	Unit 1	Unit 2	Unit 3	Unit 4	ALPHABETICAL ORDER
1.	C U Glass, Inc.	_____	_____	_____	_____	_____
2.	C O Cooking Company	_____	_____	_____	_____	_____
3.	Chas. C. Class Co.	_____	_____	_____	_____	_____
4.	Colde Mfg. Co.	_____	_____	_____	_____	_____
5.	CCC Developers	_____	_____	_____	_____	_____

Check your answers.

Filing Fact

When a label is prepared for a file folder, the personal or business name is usually written in indexing order but with the proper punctuation. A file folder label for a person might appear as *Stewart, Geo. D.* or *Davis-Farrell, Peggy.* A file folder for a business might appear as *Best & Co.* or *Jay's Sash and Glass.*

RULE 13 • Hyphenated Company Names

Hyphenated words or letters in company names (such as *Wilson-Wyatt Company* and *Now-U-C Window Company*) are considered to be one unit. They are indexed and filed as one word (without the hyphen).

	Names	Unit 1	Unit 2	Unit 3	ALPHABETICAL ORDER
1.	Upton-Manley Windmills	UptonManley	Windmills		UC Windows Inc
2.	U-Will-See Optometrists	UWillSee	Optometrists		UptonManley Windmills
3.	U-See Window Company	USee	Window	Company	UPTown Books
4.	UP-Town Books	UPTown	Books		USee Window Company
5.	U-C Windows, Inc.	UC	Windows	Inc	UWillSee Optometrists

Task Tip

In a pinch, you can use a piece of sticky-back note paper as a temporary file folder label.

Index and alphabetize the following names in the spaces provided.

Names	Unit 1	Unit 2	Unit 3
1. Bigger-Bargains Food Shoppe	_____	_____	_____
2. Biger-Fox Co.	_____	_____	_____
3. Bye-N-Buy Baby Store	_____	_____	_____
4. Big-Top Circus	_____	_____	_____
5. Bigonia-Fox Publishing	_____	_____	_____

ALPHABETICAL ORDER
_____
_____
_____
_____
_____

Check your answers.

RULE 14 • Compass Points in Company Names

Compass points (such as *North, South, Southwest,* and *North East*) in company names are indexed and alphabetized as written. For example, when indexing and filing, *North* is one unit; *North East* is two units; and *Northeast* is one unit.

Names	Unit 1	Unit 2	Unit 3	ALPHABETICAL ORDER
1. South East Binders	South	East	Binders	North Eastern Grange
2. South Park Cafe	South	Park	Cafe	Northeastern Bagels
3. Southeast Brokers	Southeast	Brokers		South East Binders
4. North Eastern Grange	North	Eastern	Grange	South Park Cafe
5. Northeastern Bagels	Northeastern	Bagels		Southeast Brokers

✔ SELF-CHECK • Exercise 14

Index and alphabetize the following names in the spaces provided.

Names	Unit 1	Unit 2	Unit 3	Unit 4
1. Northern Heat Company	_____	_____	_____	_____
2. North East Gas Co.	_____	_____	_____	_____
3. Southeast Bean Company	_____	_____	_____	_____
4. Southern Hats, Inc.	_____	_____	_____	_____
5. North South Systems	_____	_____	_____	_____

ALPHABETICAL ORDER

_____

_____

_____

_____

_____

Check your answers.

RULE 15 • Company Names with Prefixes

As with personal names, company names may include city names that contain a prefix. When indexing company names such as *San Antonio Services, Des Moines Electric Co.,* or *Los Angeles Music Store,* consider the city name as one filing unit. Common prefixes frequently found in city names are *Del, Des, El, Las, Los, St., San, Santa,* and *Terre.*

Names	Unit 1	Unit 2	Unit 3	ALPHABETICAL ORDER
1. Los Alamos Fire Shoppe	LosAlamos	Fire	Shoppe	DelMundo Restaurant
2. San Francisco Steak House	SanFrancisco	Steak	House	DesMoines Antiques
3. Santa Anita Demolition Co.	SantaAnita	Demolition	Co	LosAlamos Fire Shoppe
4. Del Mundo Restaurant	DelMundo	Restaurant		SanFrancisco Steak House
5. Des Moines Antiques	DesMoines	Antiques		SantaAnita Demolition Co

☑ SELF-CHECK • Exercise 15

Index and alphabetize the following names in the spaces provided.

Names	Unit 1	Unit 2	Unit 3
1. Des Plaines Publishing Co.	_____	_____	_____
2. Terre Haute Book Store	_____	_____	_____
3. Santa Fe Cattle Company	_____	_____	_____
4. El Paso Bus Lines	_____	_____	_____
5. San Bernadoni Fruit Growers	_____	_____	_____

ALPHABETICAL ORDER
_____
_____
_____
_____
_____

Check your answers.

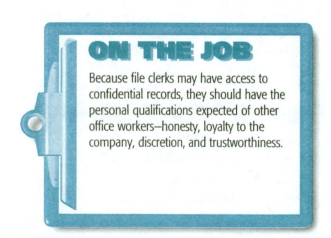

ON THE JOB

Because file clerks may have access to confidential records, they should have the personal qualifications expected of other office workers—honesty, loyalty to the company, discretion, and trustworthiness.

SELF-CHECK • Review Exercise 3

The following exercise is based on filing rules 11–15. Index and alphabetize the following names in the spaces provided.

	Names	Unit 1	Unit 2	Unit 3	Unit 4
1.	San Diego Sand Co.				
2.	Southeast Junque Store				
3.	Lane-Starr Belt Co.				
4.	LAFF Gag Store				
5.	See U Later Cafe				
6.	South West Beverages				
7.	L. L. Gaff Brokers				
8.	See-U-Later Optical Co.				
9.	Las Vegas Candy Shop				
10.	The Lolly Gag Cafe				

ALPHABETICAL ORDER

_____

_____

_____

_____

_____

_____

_____

_____

_____

_____

Check your answers.

If you had any errors in indexing or alphabetizing, refer to the rule column alongside the name in the answer section. Review the rule and make needed corrections in your answers. Be sure you understand *all* the rules.

If you made any mistakes at all, complete Self-Check Reinforcement Exercise 3, which follows.

✔ SELF-CHECK • Reinforcement Exercise 3

The following exercise is based on filing rules 11–15. Index and alphabetize the following names in the spaces provided.

Names	Unit 1	Unit 2	Unit 3	Unit 4
1. L. Briley Music Co.				
2. Look-Us-Over Decorators				
3. El Dorado Tea Co.				
4. Eastern-Day Hobby Shoppe				
5. The Lotta House Cafe				
6. Elden Crest Food Store				
7. L O T Binders				
8. East West Knit Shop				
9. Lotus Blossom Cosmetics				
10. Local Motion, Inc.				

ALPHABETICAL ORDER

_____

_____

_____

_____

_____

_____

_____

_____

_____

_____

Check your answers.

If you are sure you have mastered the first 15 rules, remove Proficiency Checkup 3 from page 91. Complete the checkup and submit it to your supervisor for evaluation. Then, with the approval of your supervisor, complete Practical Applications 4 and 5 and Fast-Find Exercise 3, which follow.

PRACTICAL APPLICATION 4

1. From the pad of cards in the envelope, remove the cards numbered 41–60. The numbers are in the upper right corner of each card. (Ignore the business letters on the back. They will be used in future activities.)
2. The names on the cards are already in correct indexing order. Arrange the cards in alphabetical order. To do this efficiently, first sort the cards into piles—one pile for each letter. Arrange the cards in each pile in alphabetical order. Then combine the piles into one pile so that all the cards are in alphabetical order. *Do not put the cards in the file box.*
3. Remove the answer sheet for Practical Application 4 from the back of this manual. List the numbers of the cards in the order in which you have arranged them.
4. Submit the answer sheet to your supervisor. Clip the cards together and place them in the large envelope until you are ready to complete Practical Application 5.

PRACTICAL APPLICATION 5

1. From the large envelope, remove the cards you used in Practical Application 4.
2. File the cards in alphabetical order in the file box with the other cards.
3. Remove the answer sheet for Practical Application 5 from the back of this manual. List the numbers of *all* the cards in the file box in the order in which you filed them.
4. Submit the answer sheet to your supervisor. *Leave the cards in the box.*

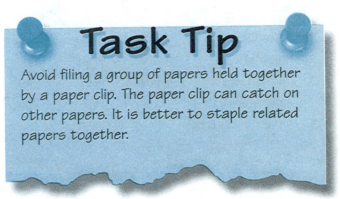

Task Tip

Avoid filing a group of papers held together by a paper clip. The paper clip can catch on other papers. It is better to staple related papers together.

FAST-FIND • Exercise 3

Complete this exercise following the instructions for Fast-Find Exercise 1 on page 14.

Names to Be Located	Number
1. The By and By Shop	_____
2. ABZ Vitality Foods	_____
3. Arturo A. DesMendez	_____
4. George W. King, III	_____
5. Dr. Henley J. Adamson	_____
6. Judge Sarah J. Barrington	_____
7. Archer Mitchell Canel	_____
8. El Santorro Mexican Cafe	_____
9. Dr. Alexander Brandon	_____
10. A A A Movers	_____

Time	
Ending Time	_____
− Beginning Time	_____
Completion Time	_____
+ Penalty Time	_____
Total Time	_____
Errors	_____

With the approval of your supervisor, begin work on Section Four.

Study the following rules and examples. Complete each self-check exercise. Then check your answers with those given in the self-check answer section on page 74. If you make any errors, review the appropriate rule and correct your errors. Be sure that you understand each rule thoroughly before going on to a new rule.

RULE 16 • Symbols in Company Names

Some businesses use symbols in their names, such as ¢ (cents), $ (dollar or dollars), + (plus), % (percent), # (pound or number), and & (and). In business names, symbols are indexed and alphabetized as though they were spelled in full. All spelled-out symbols except *and* (&) are capitalized.

	Names	Unit 1	Unit 2	Unit 3	Unit 4		ALPHABETICAL ORDER
1.	Three $ Stores	Three	Dollar	Stores			Three Cents Savings Bank
2.	Three % Flooring	Three	Percent	Flooring			Three Dollar Stores
3.	Trust & Treat Storage	Trust	and	Treat	Storage		Three Percent Flooring
4.	Three + Three Co.	Three	Plus	Three	Co		Three Plus Three Co
5.	Three ¢ Savings Bank	Three	Cents	Savings	Bank		Trust and Treat Storage

SELF-CHECK • Exercise 16

Index and alphabetize the following names in the spaces provided.

	Names	Unit 1	Unit 2	Unit 3	Unit 4
1.	Cost + Distributors				
2.	$ Rental Co.				
3.	Costner & Caffrey Realtors				
4.	Cozy # Cafe				
5.	Doller & Ryan Attorneys				

ALPHABETICAL ORDER

_____

_____

_____

_____

_____

Check your answers.

RULE 17 • Possessives and Contractions in Company Names

In company names, ignore the apostrophe in possessives (such as *Moe's Garage*) and in contractions (such as *Can't Guess Beauty Salon*). All other punctuation marks (periods, commas, dashes, hyphens, exclamation marks, and so on) are also ignored when indexing and alphabetizing company names.

	Names	Unit 1	Unit 2	Unit 3
1.	Lanny's Shoe Shop	Lannys	Shoe	Shop
2.	Luk-E-U Diner	LukEU	Diner	
3.	Luxury Lace, Ltd.	Luxury	Lace	Ltd
4.	Lonesome Cowboy's Bootery	Lonesome	Cowboys	Bootery
5.	Let's Boogie Tuxedos	Lets	Boogie	Tuxedos

ALPHABETICAL ORDER
Lannys Shoe Shop
Lets Boogie Tuxedos
Lonesome Cowboys Bootery
LukEU Diner
Luxury Lace Ltd

✔ SELF-CHECK • Exercise 17

Index and alphabetize the following names in the spaces provided.

	Names	Unit 1	Unit 2	Unit 3	Unit 4
1.	Desi's Deli	_____	_____	_____	_____
2.	Disco-Dance Fever, Inc.	_____	_____	_____	_____
3.	Dishes, Drapes, Drains, Ltd.	_____	_____	_____	_____
4.	Don't Panic Movers	_____	_____	_____	_____
5.	Dec-O-Trim Cabinetry	_____	_____	_____	_____

ALPHABETICAL ORDER
_____
_____
_____
_____
_____

Check your answers.

RULE 18 • Identical Company Names

When two or more company names are identical, the address is used to determine the correct filing order. The parts of the address are compared in the following order: (1) city or town, (2) state or province, (3) street, (4) building number in ascending numeric order.

	Names	Unit 1	Unit 2	Unit 3	Unit 4	Unit 5	Unit 6
1.	East Consultants 116 Central Avenue Highland, Colorado	East	Consultants	Highland	Colorado	Central Avenue	116
2.	East Consultants 1160 Central Avenue Highland, California	East	Consultants	Highland	California	Central Avenue	1160
3.	East Consultants 1610 Central Avenue Highland, Colorado	East	Consultants	Highland	Colorado	Central Avenue	1610
4.	Ease Builders 2316 Hanson Boulevard Highland, Texas	Ease	Builders	Highland	Texas	Hanson Boulevard	2316
5.	Ease Builders 3947 Hanson Boulevard Highland, Georgia	Ease	Builders	Highland	Georgia	Hanson Boulevard	3947

ALPHABETICAL ORDER

Ease Builders Highland Georgia 3947 Hanson Boulevard

Ease Builders Highland Texas 2316 Hanson Boulevard

East Consultants Highland California 1160 Central Avenue

East Consultants Highland Colorado 116 Central Avenue

East Consultants Highland Colorado 1610 Central Avenue

Technology in Filing

More than 75 percent of all U.S. corporations use electronic mail—e-mail. If you need to keep an e-mail message, don't print it out. Instead create subdirectories, folders, or files on your computer in which to store e-mail messages.

✔ SELF-CHECK • Exercise 18

Index and alphabetize the following names in the spaces provided.

Names	Unit 1	Unit 2	Unit 3	Unit 4	Unit 5	Unit 6
1. Cozy Cafe 2740 Leland Avenue Ames, Iowa	_____	_____	_____	_____	_____	_____
2. Cellular, Ltd. 6800 Falcon Road Rockford, Illinois	_____	_____	_____	_____	_____	_____
3. Cozy Cafe 2740 Leland Avenue Ames, Alabama	_____	_____	_____	_____	_____	_____
4. Cellular, Ltd. 117 Falcon Road Rockford, Illinois	_____	_____	_____	_____	_____	_____
5. Cozy Cafe 212 Leland Avenue Ames, Alabama	_____	_____	_____	_____	_____	_____

ALPHABETICAL ORDER

_____

_____

_____

_____

_____

Check your answers.

RULE 19 • Numbers in Company Names

Numbers in company names (such as *3 Amigos Restaurant* and *4 Corners Garage*) are *not* spelled out. These company names are filed in ascending numeric order (lowest to highest) in front of everything else in the entire file.

Hyphenated numbers (such as *6-12 Convenience Store*) are indexed and filed according to the number *before* the hyphen (the *6*); the number after the hyphen (the *12*) is disregarded.

When a company name contains an ordinal number (such as *1st, 2nd, 8th*), the *st, nd,* or *th* is ignored.

Company names starting with spelled-out numbers (such as *Ninth Street Deli*) are filed alphabetically as usual.

Names	Unit 1	Unit 2	Unit 3	Unit 4	ALPHABETICAL ORDER
1. Eighth Street Diner	Eighth	Street	Diner		8 Brothers Cafe
2. 8 Brothers Cafe	8	Brothers	Cafe		8 Travel Agency
3. 8-8-8 Travel Agency	8	Travel	Agency		9 Friends Cleaning Service
4. 10th Street Deli	10	Street	Deli		10 Street Deli
5. 9 Friends Cleaning Service	9	Friends	Cleaning	Service	Eighth Street Diner

SELF-CHECK • Exercise 19

Index and alphabetize the following names in the spaces provided.

Names	Unit 1	Unit 2	Unit 3	Unit 4	ALPHABETICAL ORDER
1. Two Tunes Music Co.	_____	_____	_____	_____	_____
2. Texas Tailors, Inc.	_____	_____	_____	_____	_____
3. Twelve Days Cafe	_____	_____	_____	_____	_____
4. 1-12 Supermarket	_____	_____	_____	_____	_____
5. 12 Trees Trailer Park	_____	_____	_____	_____	_____

Check your answers.

RULE 20 • Government Names

When names of federal government agencies are to be filed, the words "United States Government" are the first three filing units, followed by the *distinctive* name of the department, bureau, division, and so on. For example, in *Federal Bureau of Investigation*, the distinctive part of the name is *Investigation*. It would be indexed and filed as *United States Government Investigation Federal Bureau of.*

When names of state and local agencies are to be filed, the first filing units are the names of the particular local unit (such as *Indiana, Marion County*). The words *County of, City of, Department of,* and so on, are included as filing units only if they appear as part of the official name. If *of* is not part of the official name, it is not added.

Names	Unit 1	Unit 2	Unit 3	Unit 4	Unit 5	Unit 6
1. U.S. Defense Department	United	States	Government	Defense	Department	
2. United States Department of Commerce	United	States	Government	Commerce	Department	of
3. Utah Department of Public Health	Utah	Public	Health	Department	of	
4. Public Health Division, Upton County	Upton	County	Public	Health	Division	
5. Department of Public Health, Oakwood	Oakwood	Public	Health	Department	of	

ALPHABETICAL ORDER

Oakwood Public Health Department of

United States Government Commerce Department of

United States Government Defense Department

Upton County Public Health Division

Utah Public Health Department of

✔ SELF-CHECK • Exercise 20

Index and alphabetize the following names in the spaces provided.

Names	Unit 1	Unit 2	Unit 3	Unit 4	Unit 5
1. Civil Division, State of Maine	_____	_____	_____	_____	_____
2. U.S. Naval Department	_____	_____	_____	_____	_____
3. Monroe Police Department	_____	_____	_____	_____	_____
4. Montrose County Water Department	_____	_____	_____	_____	_____
5. United States Veterans Administration	_____	_____	_____	_____	_____

ALPHABETICAL ORDER

_____

_____

_____

_____

_____

Check your answers.

SELF-CHECK • Review Exercise 4

The following exercise is based on filing rules 16–20. Index and alphabetize the following names in the spaces provided.

Names	Unit 1	Unit 2	Unit 3	Unit 4	Unit 5	Unit 6
1. Utah Environmental Department						
2. Uriah's Digging Service						
3. Threatt Textiles 68 Hunt Street Lawson, Utah						
4. Underwood & Blake Co.						
5. U.S. Postal Service						
6. Ten Ton Trucks, Inc.						
7. Threatt Textiles 740 Hobson Street Lawson, Utah						
8. 10th Street Fine Foods						
9. Union City Sanitation Department						
10. Three $ Ties, Inc.						

ALPHABETICAL ORDER

_____

_____

_____

_____

_____

_____

_____

_____

_____

_____

Check your answers.

If you had any errors in indexing or alphabetizing, refer to the rule column alongside the name in the answer section. Review the rule and make needed corrections in your answers. Be sure that you understand *all* the rules.

If you made any mistakes at all, complete Self-Check Reinforcement Exercise 4, which follows.

✔ SELF-CHECK • Reinforcement Exercise 4

The following exercise is based on filing rules 16–20. Index and alphabetize the following names in the spaces provided.

	Names	Unit 1	Unit 2	Unit 3	Unit 4	Unit 5	Unit 6
1.	U.S. Defense Department						
2.	State of Mississippi Health Department						
3.	Mell's Delicatessen						
4.	$ Meal Deli						
5.	Melton's Brick Company						
6.	Ugly's Stained Furniture						
7.	Manny's Subs 16 Rose Street Millville, Ohio						
8.	Sixteen Candles Music Shop						
9.	Manny's Subs 16 Rose Street Millville, Maine						
10.	16 Motel						

ALPHABETICAL ORDER

_____

_____

_____

_____

_____

_____

_____

_____

_____

_____

Check your answers.

If you are sure you have mastered the first 20 rules, remove Proficiency Checkup 4 from page 93. Complete the checkup and submit it to your supervisor for evaluation. With the approval of your supervisor, complete Practical Applications 6 and 7 and Fast-Find Exercise 4, which follow.

PRACTICAL APPLICATION 6

1. From the pad of cards, remove the cards numbered 61–96. The numbers are in the upper right corner of each card. (Ignore the business letters on the back. These will be used in future activities.)
2. The names on the cards have already been indexed in correct order. Arrange the cards in alphabetical order. *Do not put the cards in the file box.*
3. Remove the answer sheet for Practical Application 6 from the back of this manual. List the numbers of the cards in the order in which you have arranged them.
4. Submit the answer sheet to your supervisor. Clip the cards together and place them in the large envelope until you are ready to complete Practical Application 7.

PRACTICAL APPLICATION 7

1. From the large envelope, remove the cards you used in Practical Application 6.
2. File the cards in alphabetical order in the file box with the other cards.
3. Remove the answer sheet for Practical Application 7 from the back of this manual. List the numbers of *all* the cards in the file box in the order in which you have filed them.
4. Submit the answer sheet to your supervisor. *Leave the cards in the box.*

FAST-FIND • Exercise 4

Complete this exercise following the instructions for Fast-Find Exercise 1 on page 14.

	Names to Be Located	Number	Time
1.	C-U-Shortly Adjusters	_____	Ending Time _____
2.	Kirsten's Country Curtains	_____	− Beginning Time _____
3.	The King & Queen Caterers	_____	Completion Time _____
4.	3 Senoritas Seaside Shoppe	_____	+ Penalty Time _____
5.	Tim Ignast	_____	Total Time _____
6.	Indiana State Health Department	_____	
7.	Early D. Danforth Contractors	_____	Errors _____
8.	Brother Alexander	_____	
9.	D E News Stand	_____	
10.	A-One Auto Repair Service	_____	

OPTIONAL PRACTICAL APPLICATION

If your supervisor directs you to do so, complete this Optional Practical Application as follows.

1. Remove all the cards from the file box.
2. Rearrange the cards in numerical order, from 1 to 96.
3. Put a rubber band around cards 41–96 and place them in the large envelope to be used later.
4. Turn cards 1–40 upside down so the blank lines are at the top.
5. Index the names in the list that follows. Write or type one name in correct indexing order on each card. Write or type the number of the name (97 to 136) in the upper right corner.
6. After you have written or typed all the names in correct indexing order, arrange the cards in alphabetical order.
7. Remove the answer sheet for the Optional Practical Application from page 00. List the numbers of the cards in the order in which you have arranged them.
8. Submit the answer sheet to your supervisor.
9. Turn the cards right side up. Place them in numerical order from 1 to 40 and then combine them with cards 41–96 from the large envelope. Place all the cards back in the large envelope.

Optional Practical Application Names

97. Rudy Roy Carrington
98. Luci Ching
99. Randolph H. Carey-Hoppen
100. Distefano
101. Lucy Chin
102. Dr. Damond J. Distefano
103. Diane Stefano
104. Diane T. Stefano
105. Prince Charles
106. Brother Anthony
107. B. T. Ford Co.
108. The B-L-T Sandwich Shop
109. Hope's Diamonds
110. North East Cosmetics
111. Fiery Burritos
112. Norb's Repair Shop
113. Five-of-Us Cafe
114. St. Louis Pizza, 1776 Pine Street, Buckeye, Delaware
115. Baltimore County Department of Health
116. Prince's Chicken Shack

117. Wanda Hope-Ansen
118. R. R. Carey
119. Mary T. d'Amore
120. Mrs. Damond J. DiStefano
121. Carey Hope
122. Alicine A. Ho
123. Ho Lee Dieu
124. Carrington Hope, III
125. Carrington Hope, Sr.
126. Charles A. Prince
127. Best-Foods, Inc.
128. Houser & Carrington, Inc.
129. B B B Deli
130. Best in the West Boots
131. B-B-B Barbecue, Inc.
132. Geo. R. North
133. 5 Friends Gift Shop
134. St. Louis Pizza, 83 Pine Street, Buckeye, Delaware
135. U.S. Department of State
136. B. B. Byford Community College

The names of several state government agencies follow. What is the *distinctive* name under which you might find each name in a telephone book or directory listing? (1) Office of Auditor General (2) Department of Environmental Protection (3) Public Service Commission (4) Consumer Services Division (5) Division of Recreation and Park.

With the approval of your supervisor, begin work on Unit 2.

Alphabetic Correspondence Filing

OBJECTIVES

After you have completed this unit, you will be able to

- Describe the placement of guides and folders in an alphabetic correspondence file.
- Identify incoming and outgoing correspondence.
- Inspect, index, code, sort, and file correspondence in an alphabetic filing system.
- Prepare cross-reference sheets.
- Retrieve specific correspondence from an alphabetic correspondence file.

Filing Fact

An alphabetic filing system is used in most offices. This system is better for small companies and for individual files.

Now that you have learned the basic indexing rules and have practiced filing address cards, you will learn how to file correspondence alphabetically. **Correspondence** refers to any kind of written communication carried on by a company within its offices and with other businesses, organizations, and individuals. Correspondence is usually in the form of letters. Correspondence may also include interoffice memos, résumés, and other kinds of business papers sent or received by the company. Even correspondence that has been faxed or e-mailed must be filed. The e-mail correspondence may be printed out, and the paper copy may be filed with regular correspondence. The e-mail correspondence may also be filed electronically.

Correspondence may be filed in a number of ways. The most common ways are alphabetically, geographically, by subject, or by number. Most businesses follow commonly accepted indexing and filing practices. Some, however, may follow rules that are slightly different. In every case, the employee must adapt to the company's filing procedures and practices.

In this part of the training program, you will file business correspondence alphabetically.

Before You Begin

1. Remove file guides G–H, I–J, and K–L from the file box. Place them in the large envelope. They will not be needed for this part of your training program.

Task Tip

When preparing labels for folders, use a consistent style such as all capital letters, a two-space indent, the same typeface, and so on.

2. Remove from the large envelope (or file box if you completed the Optional Practical Application on p. 101) the 96 cards you used earlier. Be sure the cards are arranged in order from 1 to 96.

3. Remove cards 85–96 from the stack. Place a clip or rubber band around these cards and put them in the large envelope. These cards will be used later.

4. Turn the cards over. Notice the business letters on the back of cards 1–80 and the four cross-reference sheets, which are numbered 14X, 26X, 37X, and 43X.

5. Arrange the letters in numeric order from 1 to 80. Place the cross-reference sheets *behind* the letters with the same numbers: 14X behind letter 14, 26X behind letter 26, and so on.

6. Place a clip or rubber band around the letters and cross-reference sheets and put them back in the large envelope until you need them.

7. From the large envelope, remove the six miniature folders. Place them behind the three remaining guides in the file box as shown in Figure 2-1.

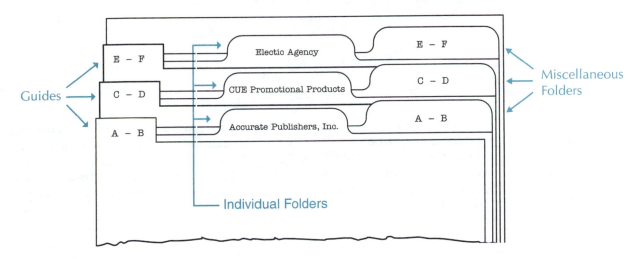

Figure 2-1

The file box should now contain the following items:

3 Primary Guides. The primary guides (A–B, C–D, E–F) show the major divisions of the alphabetic filing system. These guides are always placed before other materials—guides and folders—that fall within that alphabetic section of the file.

3 Individual Folders. Individual folders are prepared for companies with whom there is considerable correspondence. In this unit, there are individual folders for Accurate Publishers, Inc., CUE Promotional Products, and Electic Agency. Any correspondence to or from these companies is placed in these individual folders.

3 Miscellaneous Folders. Miscellaneous folders contain correspondence *from* and *to* companies, organizations, and individuals for whom there are no individual folders. An individual folder is only set up with a particular company when there is a good deal of correspondence with that company. If Reade & Relaxe Book Centers does not do a lot of business with some companies, no individual folders are needed. Letters from several different companies are filed in the same miscellaneous folder.

Task Tip

If a file folder is more than one inch thick, start a new folder.

There are many filing systems that use various arrangements of guides and folders. The system at Reade & Relaxe Book Centers and in this training program uses the combination of primary guides, individual folders, and miscellaneous folders previously described.

Filing Fact

File folders come in various "cuts." "Third cut" file folders have three tabs across the top; "fifth cut" file folders have five tabs across the top. They also come in various colors. It is best to use colored file folders for something specific. For example, green folders could signify administrative files, red folders might be personnel files, and blue folders could designate project files.

Filing Correspondence Alphabetically

Did You Know That

According to a 1994 article, it costs about $120 in labor to track down a misplaced document or $250 in labor to re-create it.

Correspondence may be classified as incoming or outgoing. **Incoming correspondence** refers to any correspondence that comes *into* the office from the outside. At Reade & Relaxe Book Centers, all incoming correspondence is stamped with the date it was received, as shown on the incoming letter in Figure 2-2. The stamped date helps establish the reasons for any delay that might have occurred.

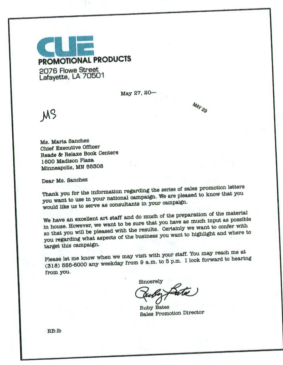

INCOMING LETTER

OUTGOING LETTER

Figure 2-2

Outgoing correspondence refers to any correspondence that begins in the Reade & Relaxe Book Centers office and is sent out to other companies or individuals. At Reade & Relaxe Book Centers, outgoing correspondence is prepared on Reade & Relaxe Book Centers letterhead stationery as shown on the outgoing letter in Figure 2-2. Copies of all outgoing correspondence are kept for filing.

In an alphabetic correspondence filing system, the steps listed below must be carefully followed if correspondence—both incoming and outgoing—is to be filed accurately and efficiently.

1. **Inspect the correspondence.** All incoming correspondence must be carefully *inspected* to see that it has been released for filing. Incoming correspondence is released for filing only after it has been read and acted on by the person or department to whom it was addressed. To show that it has been released for filing, incoming correspondence is initialed by a responsible party, usually in the upper left portion of the correspondence (see Figure 2-3). If the correspondence *does not* have release marks, it is not filed but sent back to the person or department for action.

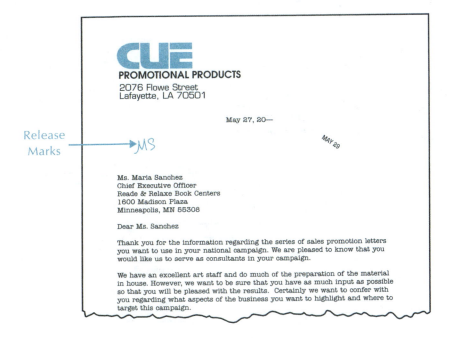

Release Marks

Figure 2-3

Outgoing correspondence does *not* have to be initialed and released for filing. Outgoing correspondence is automatically filed, without inspecting it for a release mark. Remember that all outgoing correspondence will be on Reade & Relaxe Book Centers letterhead stationery.

2. **Index the correspondence.** As in Unit 1, *indexing* means deciding the name under which you will file materials. The rules you learned in Unit 1 for indexing and filing cards also apply to correspondence. However, you must look over the correspondence to decide under which name it is to be filed. Follow these steps:

For incoming correspondence:

a. If letterhead stationery was used, file the correspondence under the company, organization, school, or government name shown in the letterhead (see Figure 2-4a).

b. If plain paper was used instead of letterhead stationery, file the correspondence under the name shown in the handwritten or typed signature (see Figure 2-4b).

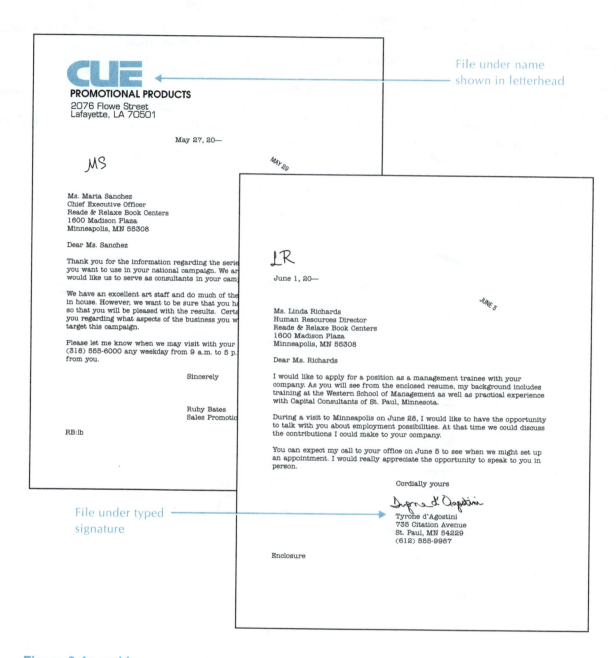

File under name shown in letterhead

File under typed signature

Figure 2-4a and b

For outgoing correspondence:

a. If the inside address contains a company, organization, school, or government name, file the correspondence under that name (see Figure 2-5a).

b. If the inside address does *not* contain a company, organization, school, or government name, file the correspondence under the name of the *person* shown in the inside address (see Figure 2-5b).

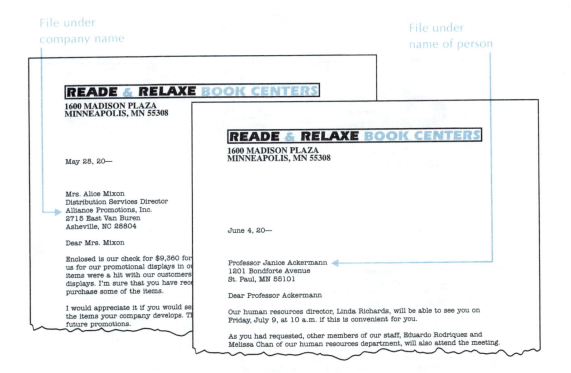

Figure 2-5a and b

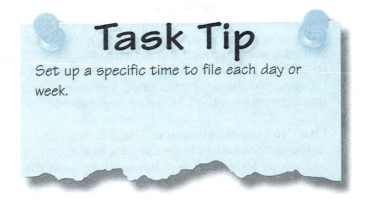

Task Tip

Set up a specific time to file each day or week.

3. **Code the correspondence.** *Coding* is marking, on the letter, the name under which the correspondence is to be filed. If someone later removes the letter from the file, the coding lets that person know the name under which it should be refiled.

   To code correspondence for filing, separate the filing units with diagonals (/) and then number the units (see Figure 2-6). For example, to code a letter from CUE Promotional Products, mark it as follows:

$$\overset{1}{\text{CUE}}/\overset{2}{\text{Promotional}}/\overset{3}{\text{Products}}$$

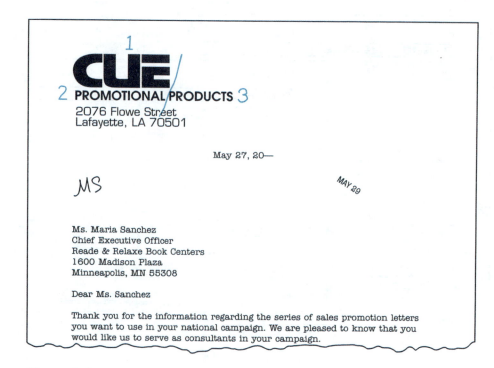

Figure 2-6

4. **Sort the correspondence.** After coding all the correspondence that is ready to be filed, sort the correspondence in alphabetical order according to the proper filing units. If you have a lot of correspondence to be filed, you may want to rough sort it first. To *rough sort* means to place the correspondence in piles according to the letters of the alphabet. After you have rough sorted the correspondence, you should fine sort it. To *fine sort* correspondence means to place the correspondence in final alphabetical order.

5. **File the correspondence.** The last step is to place the correspondence in the proper folders in the file. Place the correspondence in the folder so that the letterhead or other heading is on the left side of the folder as it faces you, as shown in Figure 2-7.

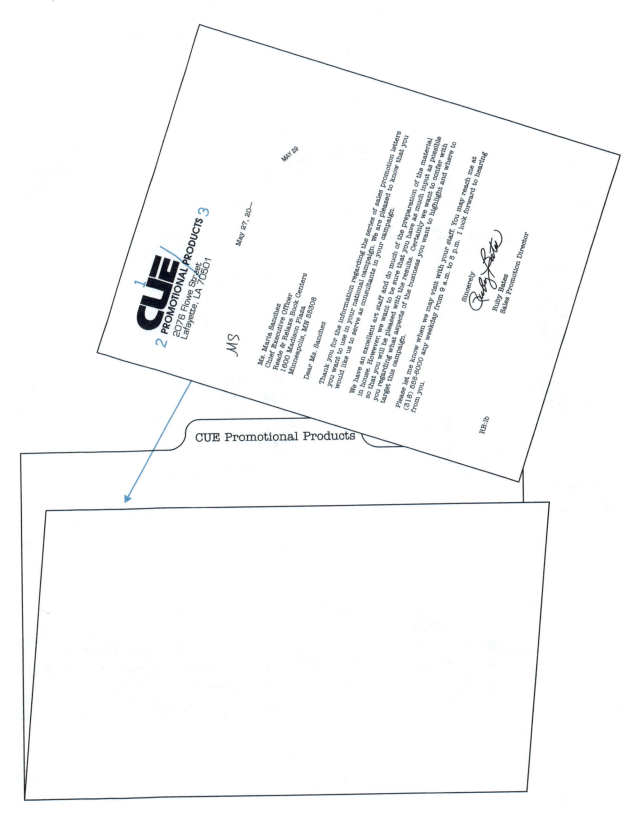

CUE Promotional Products

1
CUE
PROMOTIONAL PRODUCTS 3
2
2076 Flowe Street
Lafayette, LA 70501

May 27, 20—

MAY 29

Ms. Maria Sanchez
Chief Executive Officer
1600 Madison Plaza
Minneapolis, MN 55308

MS

Dear Ms. Sanchez

Thank you for the information regarding the series of sales promotion letters you want to use in your national campaign. We are pleased to know that you would like us to serve as consultants in your campaign.

We have an excellent art staff and do much of the preparation of the material in house. However, we want to be sure that you have as much input as possible so that you will be pleased with the results. Certainly we want to confer with you regarding what aspects of the business you want to highlight and where to target this campaign.

Please let me know when we may visit with your staff. You may reach me at (318) 555-6000 any weekday from 9 a.m. to 5 p.m. I look forward to hearing from you.

Sincerely

Ruby Bates

Ruby Bates
Sales Promotion Director

RB:ib

Figure 2-7

a. Correspondence in an *individual folder* is always arranged by date, with the most recent date in front (see Figure 2-8). Remember that only correspondence to or from one company or individual is filed in an individual folder.

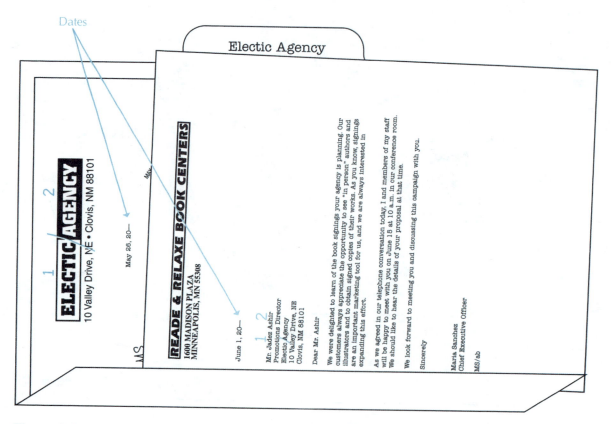

Figure 2-8

Filing Fact

"Hanging" files are suspended from the sides of a file drawer or a metal frame in the file drawer, allowing you to slide them back and forth in the drawer. They also allow you better access to file folders and prevent the folders from sliding down in a loosely filled drawer.

b. Correspondence in a *miscellaneous folder* is always arranged alphabetically. If there are two or more pieces of correspondence filed under the same name in a miscellaneous folder, the correspondence filed under that name is arranged by date, with the most recent date in front (see Figure 2-9).

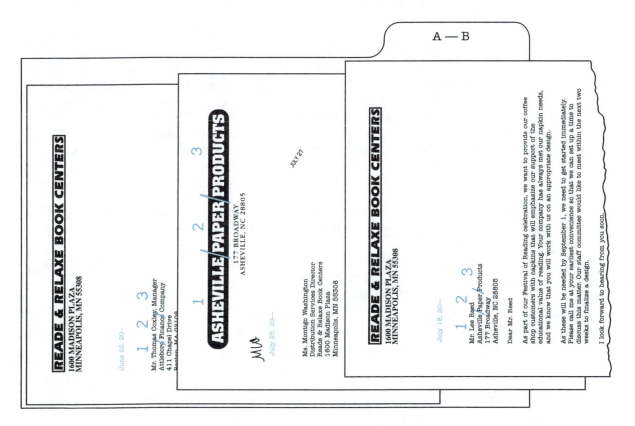

Figure 2-9

You now are ready to file some correspondence. If you need help, refer to the previous steps as you complete the exercises.

Task Tip

Move any trash off your work space (desk, table, floor) daily!

✔ SELF-CHECK • Exercise 21

1. Remove the letters numbered 1–10 from the large envelope.
2. Inspect each *incoming* letter to be sure that it has been released for filing. Remember that incoming letters are those that come from outside the Reade & Relaxe Book Centers office; they are stamped with the date they were received. Released letters have initials in the upper left corner. If you find a letter without a release mark, place a check mark under the number of the letter to show that it has *not* been released. Ordinarily, a letter that has not been released is returned to the person to whom it was addressed for action; but in these exercises, this will not be done. Keep a list (on scratch paper) of the numbers of the letters that have not been released.

   Remember that copies of *outgoing* correspondence are on Reade & Relaxe Book Centers letterhead stationery and do not have to be released. As a result, the inspecting step can be omitted.
3. Index and code each letter—both incoming and outgoing letters—according to the name under which you will file the letter. Code the letter by first separating the filing units with diagonals and then numbering the filing units.
4. Check to see if you have inspected, indexed, and coded the letters properly by comparing your answers with those for Self-Check Exercise 21 on page 83.
5. If you made any errors, review the procedures in this unit so that you will not repeat the errors.
6. Clip the letters together for use in Self-Check Exercise 22.

✔ SELF-CHECK • Exercise 22

Using letters 1–10 from Self-Check Exercise 21, complete these steps.

1. Sort the letters into stacks, one stack for each of the alphabetic groups indicated on the tabs of the primary guides: A–B, C–D, and E–F.
2. Arrange the letters in alphabetical order in each stack. If there is more than one letter for the same individual or firm, arrange these letters by date, with the most recent date on top. Use the date on the letter, not the stamped date.
3. File the letters for which there are individual folders in the proper individual folder. File the others in the miscellaneous folders.
4. Check to see if you have filed the letters properly by comparing your work with the answers for Self-Check Exercise 22 on page 84.
5. If you made any errors, review the procedures in this unit so that you will not make the same errors in future exercises.

Filing Fact

Most companies have file retention guidelines. Those guidelines cover what records should be kept, where they are stored, and how long they are stored.

Cross-Referencing

Sometimes correspondence can be filed under more than one name. If there is any doubt about which name to choose for filing a letter, a **cross-reference sheet** can be prepared. For example, if a letter to Mr. John Holston concerns the application of Mr. William Justine for a job, the letter would be filed under the name of *Holston John*. However, since the letter concerns another individual with whom the company has had correspondence, a cross-reference sheet should be prepared for that other individual, William Justine (see Figure 2-10). The cross-reference sheet would be filed under *Justine William*.

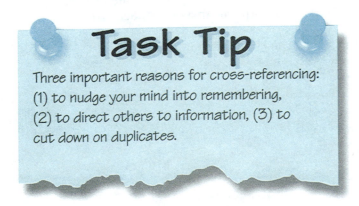

READE & RELAXE BOOK CENTERS
1600 MADISON PLAZA
MINNEAPOLIS, MN 55308

June 26, 20--

2 / 1
Mr. John Holston
1208 Lone Star Boulevard
Austin, TX 73865

Dear Mr. Holston:

2   1
X   We recently received a resume and application for employment with our company from Mr. William Justine, a former employee of yours. Mr. Justine indicated that you had consented to serve as a reference for him.

As we have been unable to reach you by telephone, we are writing to ask if you could recommend Mr. Justine for a position as a marketing research assistant. Any information you could provide us as to Mr. Justine's abilities, creativity, specific strengths and weaknesses, and general overall ability would be greatly appreciated.

If you prefer, you may call me at my office at your convenience. May we hear from you soon.

Sincerely,

Linda Richards
Human Resources Director

LR:ab

CROSS-REFERENCE SHEET

1   2
Subject _Justine, William_

Item _June 26, 20--_

ng _Application of Mr. William Justine_
for employment.

SEE

Subject _Holston, John_

Figure 2-10

Task Tip

Three important reasons for cross-referencing:
(1) to nudge your mind into remembering,
(2) to direct others to information, (3) to cut down on duplicates.

✔ SELF-CHECK • Exercise 23

In this exercise, you will inspect, index, code, sort, and file letters 11–20. You will also prepare one cross-reference sheet.

1. Remove the letters numbered 11–20 and cross-reference sheet 14X from the large envelope.

2. Inspect each *incoming letter* to be sure that it has the proper release mark. Place a check mark under the number of each letter that is not properly released. Keep a list (on scratch paper) of the numbers of any letters that have not been released. Remember that copies of outgoing correspondence will be on Reade & Relaxe letterheads and will not have release marks.

3. Index and code each letter according to the name under which you will file it. Separate the filing units with diagonals and number the filing units.

   According to the rules you have learned, letter 14 should be filed under *Bailey C. Brunson Senior High School*. However, since it is from a student, the letter might also be looked for in the files under the student's name, William C. Franz, Jr. To avoid confusion, prepare a cross-reference sheet as follows:

   a. Indicate that letter 14 will be cross-referenced under the name of William C. Franz, Jr., by underlining the name in the signature line and numbering the filing units. Place an "X" alongside the name in the margin of the letter to show that this is the cross-reference caption.

   b. Complete the cross-reference sheet (numbered 14X) by writing *Franz William C Jr* on the Name or Subject line; code by separating the units with diagonals and numbering the filing units. Write *June 2, 20—* (the date of the letter) on the Date line; *Request for judging and speaker for high school class* on the Regarding line; and *Bailey C Brunson Senior High School* on the See Name or Subject line.

   c. The letter will be filed under *Bailey C Brunson Senior High School*; the cross-reference sheet will be filed under *Franz William C Jr.*

4. Sort all the letters and the cross-reference sheet into stacks, one stack for each of the alphabetic groups on the tabs of the primary guides: A–B, C–D, and E–F.

5. Within each stack, arrange the letters in alphabetical order.

6. File the letters and the cross-reference sheet in the proper individual and miscellaneous folders. Remember to arrange letters in *individual folders* by the date on the letter (not the stamped date), latest date in front. In the *miscellaneous folders*, make sure that you have placed the letters in alphabetical order with those already in the folders. If there is more than one letter for a name in a miscellaneous folder, arrange those letters by date, with the most recent date in front.

7. Check to see whether you have inspected, indexed, and filed the letters properly by comparing your work with the answers for Self-Check Exercise 23 on page 84.

8. If you made any errors, review the procedures in this unit.

9. Now go on to Self-Check Exercise 24.

✔ SELF-CHECK • Exercise 24

Filing correspondence accurately is only half the job in any filing system. You must be able to *retrieve* or find the correspondence quickly when it is needed.

See how quickly and accurately you can find the following letters. Complete the table as you locate the letters in the file box. Be sure to put the letters back in their proper places in the file.

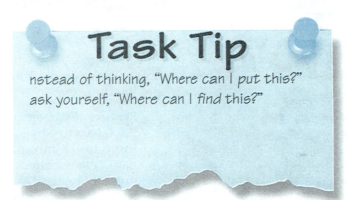

	Letter Requested	Letter Number	Folder Caption	Filed Behind Letter	Filed in Front of Letter
0.	Letter from The Aviator Magazine June 1	17	A–B	9	20
1.	Letter from A-Z Market Research June 1	_____	_____	_____	_____
2.	Letter from Tyrone d'Agostini June 1	_____	_____	_____	_____
3.	Letter from Eversoll's Bakery May 26	_____	_____	_____	_____
4.	Letter from William C. Franz, Jr. June 2	_____	_____	_____	_____
5.	Letter from Delvecca Distributors, Inc. May 27	_____	_____	_____	_____

Check your work against the answers for Self-Check Exercise 24 on page 84. Make sure you correct and understand any errors you made. Then go on to Self-Check Exercise 25.

Filing Fact

Correspondence or other materials are sometimes filed in chronological order. A *tickler file* is one example of a chronological file that usually has 12 large folders or dividers, one for each month. A tickler file also has 31 smaller folders, one for each day of the month. Items that need attention are filed in the appropriate day folder within the month folder/divider. When each day's items are taken care of, the day folder is moved to the next month.

Technology in Filing

On a computer, if you don't deliberately decide where to file something when you save it, your computer may make the decision for you. That may result in a misfiled document that can be very difficult to find.

✔ SELF-CHECK • Exercise 25

In this exercise, you will inspect, index, code, sort, and file letters 21–30. You will also prepare one cross-reference sheet. Follow these steps in completing this exercise.

1. Remove the letters numbered 21–30 and cross-reference sheet 26X from the large envelope.
2. Inspect each incoming letter to be sure that it has the proper release mark. Place a check mark under the number of each letter that is not properly released. Keep a list (on scratch paper) of the numbers of those letters that have not been released. Remember that copies of outgoing correspondence will be on Reade & Relaxe Book Centers letterhead stationery and will not have release marks.
3. Index and code each letter according to the name under which you will file the letter. Separate the units with diagonals and number the filing units. Prepare a cross-reference sheet for letter 26 as follows:
   a. Indicate that you are cross-referencing this letter under the name *Jessica Bradley* by underlining the name in the letter. Number the filing units. Place an "X" alongside the name in the margin of the letter to indicate that this is the cross-reference caption.
   b. Complete the cross-reference sheet (numbered 26X) by writing *Bradley Jessica* on the Name or Subject line; code by separating the units with diagonals and numbering the filing units. Write *June 2, 20—* (the date of the letter) on the Date line; *Questions about human resources career* on the Regarding line; and *Alamance Community College* on the See Name or Subject line.
   c. The letter will be filed under *Alamance Community College;* the cross-reference sheet will be filed under *Bradley Jessica.*
4. Sort the letters and the cross-reference sheet into stacks, one stack for each of the alphabetic groups indicated on the tabs of the primary guides: A–B, C–D, and E–F.
5. Within each stack, arrange the letters in alphabetical order.
6. File the letters and the cross-reference sheet in the proper individual and miscellaneous folders. Remember to arrange letters in *individual folders* by the typed date, latest date in front. In the *miscellaneous folders,* make sure that you have placed the letters in alphabetical order with those already in the folders. If there is more than one piece of correspondence for the name in a miscellaneous folder, arrange those letters by date, with the most recent date in front.
7. Check to see if you have inspected, indexed, and filed the letters properly by comparing your work with the answers for Self-Check Exercise 25 on page 84.
8. If you made any errors, review the procedures in this unit.
9. Now go on to Self-Check Exercise 26.

✔ SELF-CHECK • Exercise 26

Using the letters in the file box, see how accurately you can locate the letters requested. Complete the table as you locate the letters. Be sure to put the letters back in their proper places in the file.

Letter Requested	Letter Number	Folder Caption	Filed Behind Letter	Filed in Front of Letter
0. Letter from Tyrone d'Agostini June 1	15	C–D	4	25
1. Letter to Accurate Publishers, Inc. June 1	_____	_____	_____	_____
2. Letter to Alliance Promotions, Inc. May 28	_____	_____	_____	_____
3. Letter from CUE Promotional Products May 27	_____	_____	_____	_____
4. Letter to Eversoll's Bakery June 1	_____	_____	_____	_____
5. Letter from The Drexel Company May 25	_____	_____	_____	_____

Check your work against the answers for Self-Check Exercise 26 on page 85. Make sure you correct and understand any errors you made. Then go on to Practical Application 8.

PRACTICAL APPLICATION 8

In this application, you are to inspect, index, code, sort, and file letters 31–50. You will also prepare two cross-reference sheets. Follow these steps:

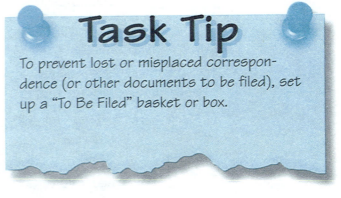

Task Tip

To prevent lost or misplaced correspondence (or other documents to be filed), set up a "To Be Filed" basket or box.

1. Remove the letters and cross-reference sheets numbered 31–50 from the large envelope.
2. Inspect each incoming letter for release marks. Place a check mark under the number of each letter not properly released. Keep a list (on scratch paper) of the numbers of those letters that have not been released.
   Remember that copies of outgoing correspondence will be on Reade & Relaxe Book Centers letterhead stationery and will not have release marks.
3. Index and code each letter.
4. Prepare cross-reference sheets for letters 37 and 43 as follows:
   a. Letter 37 will be cross-referenced under Jennifer Drexler. Indicate that you are cross-referencing this letter by underlining Jennifer Drexler's name in the letter. Place an "X" alongside the name in the margin of the letter to indicate that this is the cross-reference caption. Number the filing units. Complete a cross-reference sheet using the information in the letter. The letter will be filed under *Clarion High School* and the cross-reference sheet under *Drexler Jennifer.*
   b. Letter 43 will be cross-referenced under Anson d'Amato. Indicate that you are cross-referencing this letter by underlining Anson d'Amato's name in the letter. Place an "X" alongside the name in the margin of

the letter to indicate that this is the cross-reference caption. Number the filing units. Complete a cross-reference sheet using the information in the letter. The letter will be filed under *Bailey Technical College* and the cross-reference sheet under *dAmato Anson.*

5. Sort the letters and cross-reference sheets.

6. File the letters and cross-reference sheets in the proper folders. Arrange letters in *individual folders* by date. In the *miscellaneous folders,* make sure that all correspondence is in correct alphabetical order. If there is more than one piece of correspondence for the same name in a miscellaneous folder, arrange the correspondence for that name by date, with the most recent date in front.

7. Remove the answer sheet for Practical Application 8 from the back of this manual. Write your name and the date in the proper blanks. Complete the answer sheet and turn it in to your supervisor for evaluation.

Now go on to Fast-Find Exercise 5 below.

FAST-FIND • Exercise 5

Complete this exercise, following the instructions for Fast-Find Exercise 1 on page 14.

Names To Be Located	Number
1. Letter from CU Productions dated May 28	_____
2. Letter from Aston Daily News dated May 28	_____
3. Letter to Alliance Promotions, Inc., dated May 28	_____
4. Letter to CUE Promotional Products dated June 2	_____
5. Letter to The Clairfield Hotel dated June 4	_____
6. Letter from William C. Franz, Jr., dated June 2	_____
7. Letter from The Crockery Shoppe dated May 27	_____
8. Letter from A-Z Market Research dated May 27	_____
9. Letter to Eleve Coffee Suppliers dated June 3	_____
10. Letter from Jessica Bradley dated June 2	_____

Time	
Ending Time	_____
− Beginning Time	_____
Completion Time	_____
+ Penalty Time	_____
Total Time	_____
Errors	_____

For which, if any, of the following names would you recommend that cross-reference sheets be prepared? (1) Jan Hunt (Mrs. Kevin), (2) NASA, (3) Wilma Sinclair-Smith, (4) E. S. Wright & Sons, Inc., (5) Wen Jonge Wu

With the approval of your supervisor, begin work on Unit 3.

Geographic Filing

OBJECTIVES

After you have completed this unit, you will be able to

▶ Explain how a geographic filing system differs from an alphabetic filing system.

▶ Inspect, index, code, sort, and file correspondence in a geographic filing system.

Did You Know That ......

By one estimate, the annual cost of maintaining a 5-drawer filing cabinet in an office is $2,099. That figure includes amounts for clerical salary and benefits, floor space, supplies, and the amortized cost of the cabinet itself.

At Reade & Relaxe Book Centers, the Promotions Department maintains a **geographic filing system,** a system in which correspondence is filed according to the *location* of the company or person named. Using such a system, Reade & Relaxe Book Centers can easily see the extent of the company's promotional campaigns and the companies in each region that Reade & Relaxe Book Centers uses to develop its promotional campaigns.

In the Promotions Department's geographic filing system, materials are filed first by *state,* then by *city,* and then by *company* or *individual* name. Figure 3-1 shows the "A" file drawer in the department's geographic filing system. Notice that the *file guides* list state names and the *file folders* list city names.

In this geographic filing system, for example, a letter from the Sunshine Agency in Tucson, Arizona, would be filed behind the *Arizona* guide in the *Tucson* folder. If there were letters from several customers in the Tucson folder, the letters would be filed in alphabetical order by the name of the company or individual.

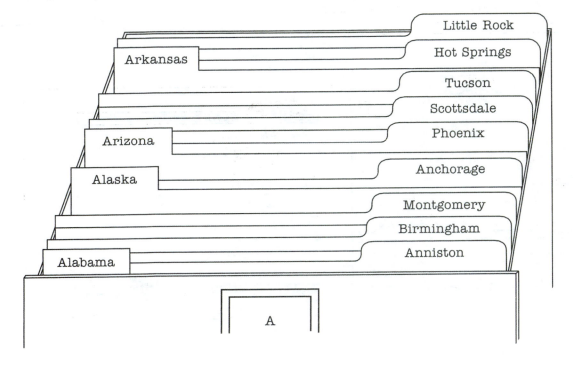

Figure 3-1

As in alphabetical correspondence filing, you must *inspect, index, code, sort,* and *file* the letters. There are several ways to code letters in a geographic filing system. One common way—the method used by Reade & Relaxe Book Centers—is as follows. Circle and number the name of the state and city; then underline the name of the company or individual, separating the units with diagonals; then number the units. You can see this method in Figure 3-2.

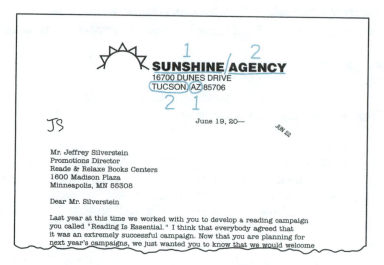

Figure 3-2

In filing this letter, you would use only the circled units—*Arizona* and *Tucson*—unless there were other letters filed under Arizona, Tucson. In that case, you would use the company name, *Sunshine Agency,* to decide on the alphabetical order of the letters in the file.

Figure 3-3 illustrates how to code letters for the geographic filing system at Reade & Relaxe Book Centers.

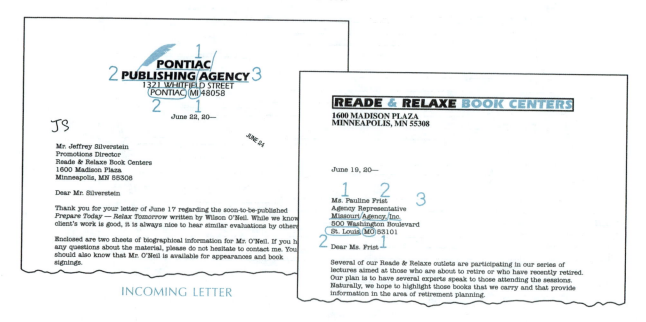

INCOMING LETTER   OUTGOING LETTER

Figure 3-3

PRACTICAL APPLICATION 9

In this exercise, you will inspect, index, code, and sort 15 letters for the geographic filing system used at Reade & Relaxe Book Centers. Follow these steps:

1. Remove the letters numbered 51–65 from the set envelope.
2. Inspect each incoming letter for release marks. Place a check mark under the number of each incoming letter that is not properly released. Keep a list (on scratch paper) of the numbers of those letters that have not been released. Copies of outgoing correspondence will be on Reade & Relaxe Book Centers letterhead stationery and will not have release marks.
3. Index and code each letter as indicated below.
   For incoming letters:
   a. Circle and number the state and city in the letterhead.
   b. Underline and number the filing units in the name of the company in the letterhead, separating the units with diagonals.
   For outgoing letters:
   a. Circle and number the state and city in the inside address.
   b. Underline and number the filing units in the name of the company in the inside address, separating the units with diagonals.
4. Sort and arrange the letters alphabetically as follows:
   a. Arrange the letters alphabetically by state. Consider the state names to be spelled in full as you alphabetize. (If necessary, refer to the chart of state abbreviations on page 112.)
   b. If there is more than one letter within a state, arrange the letters alphabetically by city.
   c. If there is more than one letter within a city, arrange the letters alphabetically by the name of the company.
   d. If there is more than one letter to or from the same company, arrange these letters by *typed date,* most recent date in front.
   e. *Do not file the letters.* Simply arrange them as instructed as though you were going to file them.
5. Remove the answer sheet for Practical Application 9 from the back of this manual. Write your name and the date in the proper blanks. Complete the answer sheet and turn it in to your supervisor. Place the letters behind all the others in the file box. *Do not file the letters in a folder.*

The Public Works Department of the city of Coral Point mows vacant lots every 8 weeks so that the city looks attractive and debris doesn't build up in overgrown lots. The city then bills lot owners for the service. How might the Public Works Department set up a geographic filing system (file guides and folders)?

With the approval of your supervisor, go on to Unit 4.

Filing Fact

The phrase *central files* usually refers to a specific location—such as a file room or a large bank of file cabinets—where everyone files information that is of use to the department.

Subject Filing

After you have completed this unit, you will be able to

- Explain how a subject filing system differs from an alphabetic filing system.
- Inspect, index, code, sort, and file correspondence in a subject filing system.

Sometimes it is much more efficient to have all the correspondence about a particular subject filed in one folder rather than in separate individual alphabetic folders. For example, it is much more convenient to have all the correspondence about reference books filed in one folder than to file the correspondence about reference books under the names of the individual suppliers.

The Distribution Services Department of Reade & Relaxe Book Centers maintains a **subject filing system.** All correspondence is filed alphabetically by subject. A chart of the primary and secondary subject headings is kept in a handy place in the department so that those who file and retrieve materials can easily decide under which caption a particular piece of correspondence is to be filed. Part of that chart is shown in Figure 4-1.

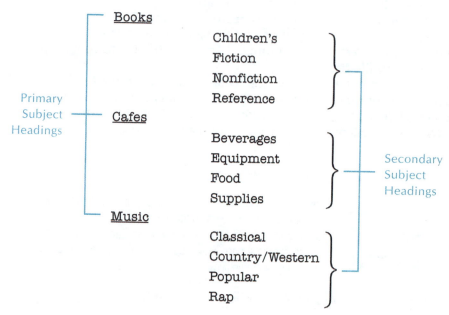

Figure 4-1

Figure 4-2 shows part of a file drawer in the subject filing system used by the Distribution Services Department. As you can see, the file guides indicate the primary headings *Books, Cafes,* and *Music.* In the Books section, file folders reflect the secondary headings—*Children's, Fiction, Nonfiction,* and *Reference.*

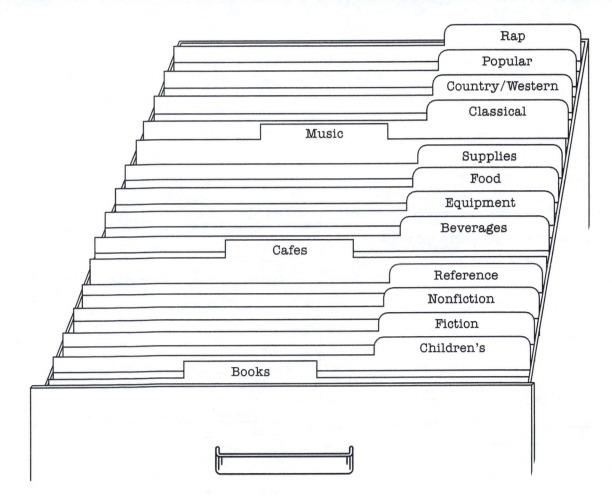

Figure 4-2

After each letter has been inspected for release marks, it is read to determine the subject under which it will be filed. For example, look at the incoming letter in Figure 4-3. Since this letter relates to a book of fiction

Figure 4-3

(a novel), the heading *Books—Fiction* is written at the top of the letter. The letter was then indexed and coded according to the name of the company sending the letter, as is done in an alphabetic correspondence filing system.

The letters in Figure 4-4 provide additional examples of correspondence that has been inspected, indexed, and coded for the subject filing system.

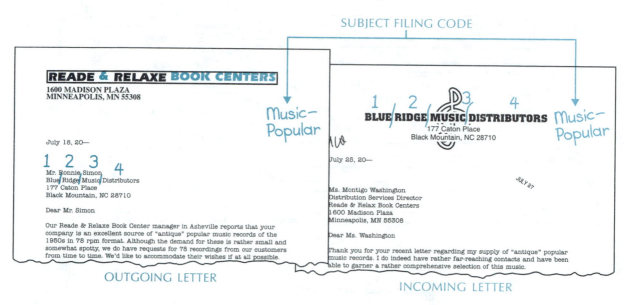

Figure 4-4

After the correspondence has been indexed and coded, the letters are sorted, first by the primary subject heading and then by the secondary subject heading. The letters are then filed in the correct folders in alphabetical order by the name of the individual or company sending or receiving them. If there are several letters to or from the same company or individual in a folder, the letters are filed by date, with the most recent date in front.

PRACTICAL APPLICATION 10

In this exercise, you will inspect, read, index, code, and sort 15 letters for the subject filing system used by the Distribution Services Department of Reade & Relaxe Book Centers. Follow these steps:

1. Remove the letters numbered 66–80 from the large envelope.
2. Inspect each incoming letter for release marks. Place a check mark under the number of each incoming letter not properly released. Keep a list (on scratch paper) of the numbers of those letters that have not been released. Remember that copies of outgoing correspondence will be on Reade & Relaxe Book Centers letterhead stationery and will not have release marks.
3. Read, index, and code each letter.
   a. Read the letter to determine the primary and secondary subject headings under which it will be filed. Refer to the chart of primary and secondary subject headings in Figure 4-1 on page 62 as needed.

b. Write the primary and secondary subject headings in the upper right corner of the letter.

c. Index and code the name of the company in the letterhead on *incoming* letters. Index and code the name of the company appearing in the inside address on *outgoing* letters.

4. Sort the letters.

a. Sort first into three piles, one for each *primary* subject heading. Refer to the chart in Figure 4-1 as needed.

b. For each primary heading pile, sort the letters alphabetically by *secondary* subject heading.

c. If there are letters from more than one company within a secondary subject heading, arrange them in alphabetical order by the name of the company.

d. If there is more than one letter from the same company under a secondary subject heading, arrange the letters from this company by the *typed date*, latest date in front.

5. Remove the answer sheet for Practical Application 10 from the back of this manual. Write your name and the date in the proper blanks. Complete the answer sheet and turn it in to your supervisor.

6. Place the letters behind all others in the file. *Do not file the letters.*

 You have recently become interested in cooking and have collected a number of recipes. Right now those recipes are in a large manila envelope. How might you file your recipes if you could use only five primary headings? What secondary headings could you use?

With the approval of your supervisor, go on to Unit 5.

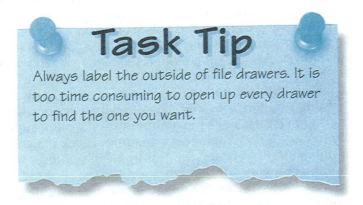

Task Tip

Always label the outside of file drawers. It is too time consuming to open up every drawer to find the one you want.

Numeric Filing

OBJECTIVES

After you have completed this unit, you will be able to

▶ Explain when a numeric filing system might be used.

▶ File index cards in a terminal digit numeric filing system.

Did You Know That

Over 90 *billion* documents are produced in this country every year; active office files grow about 25 percent every 3–4 years; record-keeping costs double every year.

Filing Fact

A numeric filing system works well for records that can be filed by policy number, product number, patient billing number, customer account number, and telephone number.

Depending on the nature of their business, some companies prefer to use a **numeric filing system** in which correspondence or other materials are filed by number. For example, insurance companies may file their correspondence according to the policy numbers assigned to customers. Publishing companies may file their correspondence by the ZIP codes of subscribers. Tax records are often filed by a citizen's social security number.

Reade & Relaxe Book Centers recently formed a Training Division to provide additional training for its employees. One way in which the Training Division does this is by providing video cassettes to help employees improve their skills in communications, sales, supervision, and telephone usage. The employees sometimes check out the videos to view them at home. At other times, the Training Division uses the videos in specific training programs for new employees.

When the video cassettes are prepared, each master copy is assigned a six-digit number corresponding to the date on which it was completed. The date is shown in military style, that is, in day-month-year order. For example, July 14, 2001, would be shown as 14-07-01. See Figure 5-1. Notice that a "0" (zero) appears before a single-digit day, month, or year.

After the cassettes are labeled with the assigned numbers, they are filed in a storage cabinet using Reade & Relaxe Book Centers' terminal digit numeric filing system. The video cassettes are arranged in the storage cabinet with the most recent date in front. In a **terminal digit numeric system,** the numbers are considered from *right to left* instead of the normal left-to-right way. For example, a video labeled *14-09-00* (September 14, 2000) would be filed in front of a video labeled *14-09-99* (September 14, 1999).

Figure 5-1

An **index card control file** is also kept to help locate particular video cassettes quickly. An index card is prepared for each video showing the six-digit number set assigned to it, its general category (*Company Policies, Customer Relations, Supervision,* or *Telephone Usage*), and the title of the video cassette. The cards in the index card control file are then filed (1) alphabetically by the general category and (2) numerically using the assigned six-digit number sets. Figure 5-2 shows the index card prepared for one of the video cassettes and where it would be placed in the index card control file. Using the index card control file, employees in the Training Division can easily locate a particular cassette in the storage cabinet.

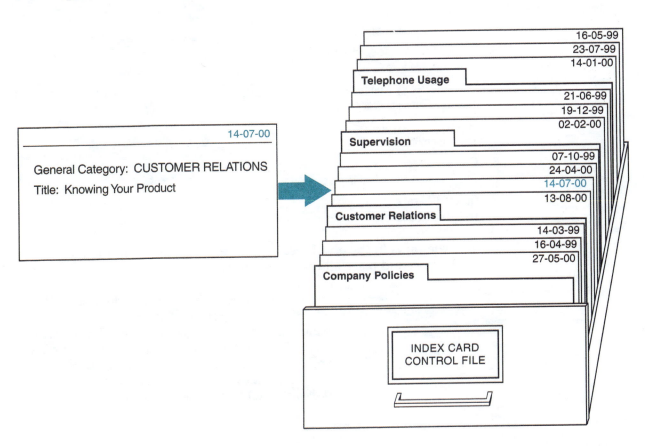

Figure 5-2

PRACTICAL APPLICATION 11

1. Remove cards numbered 85–96 from the envelope. Turn the cards over. You will notice that index cards have already been prepared for the 12 video cassettes produced by the Training Division. Each card lists the six-digit number assigned to the video cassette, the general category, and the video's title.

2. Sort the index cards alphabetically first by the general categories: *Company Policies, Customer Relations, Supervision,* and *Telephone Usage.*

3. Within each of the four stacks, arrange the cards in numeric order by the assigned six-digit numbers. Consider the digits from *right to left;* that is, consider first the year, then the month, and finally the day. Note that if the last two digits of the assigned number are "00" or "01," the year date is "2000" or "2001."

4. Combine the four stacks of cards, keeping the general categories in alphabetical order.

5. Remove the answer sheet for Practical Application 11. List the numbers of the cards in the order in which you have arranged them.

6. Submit the answer sheet to your supervisor. Place the cards in the envelope until you are ready to complete Fast-Find Exercise 6.

FAST-FIND • Exercise 6

Remove the index cards 81–92, which you used in Practical Application 11, from the set envelope. Complete this exercise following the instructions for Fast-Find Exercise 1 on page 14.

Cards to Be Located	Number		Time
1. General Category: Customer Relations Title: Satisfying the Customer	_____	Ending Time	_____
2. General Category: Company Policies Title: The Benefits Program	_____	− Beginning Time	_____
3. General Category: Telephone Usage Title: Handling Irate Customers	_____	Completion Time	_____
4. General Category: Company Policies Title: The Company Policy Manual	_____	+ Penalty Time	_____
5. General Category: Supervision Title: Communicating with Employees	_____	Total Time	_____
6. General Category: Customer Relations Title: Making a Good First Impression	_____		
7. General Category: Supervision Title: Helping Employees Grow	_____	Errors	_____

Place the cards in the envelope. Remove all materials from the file box. Flatten the box, and place all the materials in the set envelope.

Suppose you have been asked to set up a numeric filing system for the following groups. On what type of number, including a separate account number, might each numeric filing system be based? (1) The local library, (2) the purchasing department of a large corporation, (3) the Payroll Department of a small company, (4) a local cable television provider, (5) a small women's clothing store, (6) a national news magazine

If your supervisor approves, go on to Unit 6.

Filing Documents Electronically

OBJECTIVES

After you have completed this unit, you will be able to

- Compare and contrast a paper filing system with an electronic filing system.
- Define *parallel files.*
- Establish a set of directories/folders that might be used within an electronic filing system and file letters within that system.

When computers first became commonplace, many people thought that we would no longer use written correspondence, forms, and so on, to carry on business and that we would carry on all of our business electronically. While the paperless office many predicted has not come to pass, today's businesses store many documents electronically—either on the computer or on computer disks and tapes—rather than in printed form. Such documents include e-mail, correspondence prepared with word processing software, and electronically completed forms. Searching for one file among the thousands stored on a computer could be extremely time-consuming. Electronically stored documents must be filed logically and consistently so that they too can be retrieved quickly and efficiently.

Creating Directories and Subdirectories

The key to filing and retrieving electronically stored documents is to create an orderly system of directories and subdirectories that make sense. A *directory* (*folder* in Microsoft Word) is a list of files. If you think of the computer's hard drive as a filing cabinet, directories/folders are the drawers of the filing cabinet. The directories/folders can hold applications programs like Windows or WordPerfect, or they can hold all of the files related to a specific category of documents.

Technology in Filing

The value of a computer is that it allows you to use a file again. If you don't intend to use the document again, there is no value in storing it in a computer.

ON THE JOB

Job titles vary. For those interested in a job in records management, job titles include file clerk, records clerk, records management director, forms analyst, records center supervisor, records systems analyst, records and microfilm manager, records administrator, and information/records manager.

Within a file cabinet drawer, file guides and file folders help to organize the materials. The file guides and folders of a computer directory are the subdirectories and files. *Subdirectories* (*subfolders* in Microsoft Word) are the categories established to group similar types of documents. For example, a directory/folder titled MYDOCUMENTS might be created to hold all word processing documents. Within that directory/folder, there might be subdirectories/subfolders with such names as BUDGETS, FORMS, LETTERS, and REPORTS. Subdirectories/folders can be several layers deep. Note too that it is not necessary for all of the directories/folders to have the same number of subdirectories.

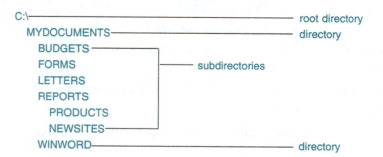

Within the subdirectories/subfolders are the *files,* the file folders of the computer system. A file may hold one document or several related documents. For example, in the BUDGETS subdirectory/subfolder, there might be the following files:

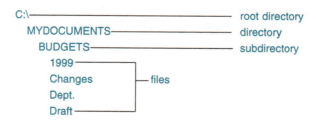

Naming Files

Every file must have a name, the electronic equivalent of a paper system's file folder label. A filename has two parts: a *root name* (which can be from one to eight characters) and an *extension* of up to three letters. Filenames should somehow reflect the file's contents and make it relatively easy to locate the file later. (Subdirectories also help greatly.)

The eight characters in a filename can be either letters or numbers. Filenames cannot, however, include any of the following characters: / (forward slash), \ (backslash), < (less than), > (greater than), * (asterisk), ? (question mark), : (colon), or ; (semicolon). In addition, there should be no spaces in a filename.

Most word processing programs automatically assign a three-character extension to the filename. In some programs, you can change the three letters for better identification. In WordPerfect, you can use the extension to help identify the file by, for example, keying "LTR" for letter. MS Word automatically assigns a final three-letter extension of *doc* to identify the file as a Word document. However, you can also assign an interval extension to further identify the file. For example, you can save the document as *xxx.ht.doc.*

Technology in Filing

Windows Explorer and File Manager will let you see all of the programs and files on your computer.

All of the filing rules presented in *Filing Made Easy, Fourth Edition,* apply to the names given to files on the computer. There are, however, two exceptions you should be aware of.

The computer reads Roman-numeral seniority designations as capital letters. "II" would thus be read as two capital letter I's instead of the Roman numeral for "two." If you use a seniority title in a filename, you must change the Roman numeral to an Arabic number; that is, "II" would become "2," "III" would become "3," and so on.

If you use numbers in filenames, the number of digits used must be the same for all similar files. Using the same number of digits ensures that the filenames are sorted in the correct order. For example, suppose you had the following two files: *4Road* and *22Road.* The computer reads the numbers from left to right and would place the two files in this order: *22Road* and *4Road.* To ensure that the files are in correct numerical order, use the same number of digits: *04Road* and *22Road.*

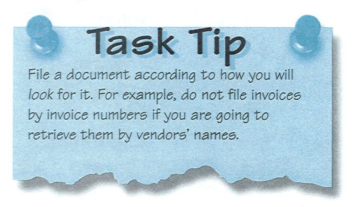

Task Tip

File a document according to how you will *look* for it. For example, do not file invoices by invoice numbers if you are going to retrieve them by vendors' names.

Electronic Filing Systems

The system of directories/folders, subdirectories/subfolders, and files presented earlier in this discussion is similar to a subject filing system. However, all of the filing systems discussed in *Filing Made Easy, Fourth Edition*—alphabetic, geographic, subject, and numeric—can be used to organize files on the computer.

Many office workers today use a system of **parallel files;** that is, the electronic filing system parallels or corresponds to the paper filing system. For example, if the company or a department of a company uses a subject filing system for its paper files, the office workers in the company or department use a subject filing system for their electronic files. The names of directories, subdirectories, and files (folders, subfolders, and files) are the same for both types of records. Employees can easily file and find records without having to remember which system is used for paper files and which system is used for electronic files.

Filing Fact

If you have a filing system that is not working well or if you have inherited it from someone else (whether it is in a file cabinet or in your computer), it is usually best to start over. It will be easier to find what you want when you need it if you have a filing system that works for you.

In this exercise, you will establish a set of subdirectories/subfolders for several pieces of correspondence. Remove the following letters from the large envelope: 51, 54, 56, 57, 58, 59, 61, 62, 65. These letters were written by Jeffrey Silverstein and earlier filed in the Promotions Department's geographic filing system. *Using only these letters,* indicate the parallel subdirectories/subfolders that would be used if these letters were filed electronically in the department. The word processing software used by the department allows subdirectory/subfolder names of more than 8 characters. In your answers, indicate that the root directory is "C:\" and the directory/folder is "Letters." Do *not* assign filenames.

1. Letter 51: _____
2. Letter 54: _____
3. Letter 56: _____
4. Letter 57: _____
5. Letter 58: _____
6. Letter 59: _____
7. Letter 61: _____
8. Letter 62: _____
9. Letter 65: _____

Check your answers. When you have finished, replace the letters in the correct order with the other letters. Place the letters in the large envelope.

Suppose you have written several letters on your computer and now want to save them. Your word processing program allows filenames of only 8 characters (plus a 3-letter extension). What filename would you assign to a letter to the *U.S. News & World Report* magazine inquiring about student subscriptions? How about a letter to Ohio University asking for admission information?

Unless your supervisor has additional exercises for you, this completes your training program. If you have successfully completed the program and demonstrated a basic knowledge of filing rules and systems, your supervisor will award you a proficiency certificate.

Answers to Self-Check Exercises

✔ SELF-CHECK • Exercise 1a

	Unit 1	Unit 2	Unit 3	ALPHABETICAL ORDER
1.	Grimm	Jane	Alice	Gilley Richard R
2.	Grimm	Jane	Ann	Gilley Richard T
3.	Gilley	Richard	R	Grayson Faith Ann
4.	Grayson	Faith	Ann	Grimm Jane Alice
5.	Gilley	Richard	T	Grimm Jane Ann

✔ SELF-CHECK • Exercise 1b

	Unit 1	Unit 2	Unit 3	ALPHABETICAL ORDER
1.	Massey	Raoul		Massey Ralph
2.	Massey	Ralph		Massey Raoul
3.	Massey	Rolly	A	Massey Rolly A
4.	Quiroga	Arturo	A	Quiroga Arturo A
5.	Quirroga	Arthur	X	Quirroga Arthur X

✔ SELF-CHECK • Exercise 2

	Unit 1	Unit 2	Unit 3	ALPHABETICAL ORDER
1.	Hay	Charro		Hanes Susie
2.	Hayes	Teddy		Hay Charro
3.	Hay	Chas	Ray	Hay Chas Ray
4.	Hayes	Thos		Hayes Teddy
5.	Hanes	Susie		Hayes Thos

✔ SELF-CHECK • Exercise 3

	Unit 1	Unit 2	Unit 3	ALPHABETICAL ORDER
1.	Franko	Mannie		Franko M
2.	Franko	M		Franko Mannie
3.	Orville	David	T	Orville
4.	Orville			Orville D
5.	Orville	D		Orville David T

✔ SELF-CHECK • Exercise 4

	Unit 1	Unit 2	Unit 3		ALPHABETICAL ORDER
1.	LaDona	Andrew	A		LaDona Andrew A
2.	StIverson	Martha	F		LaSalle Ann
3.	LaSalle	Ann			ODonald Ruth Ann
4.	ODonald	Ruth	Ann		ODonnell Randolph A
5.	ODonnell	Randolph	A		StIverson Martha F

✔ SELF-CHECK • Exercise 5

	Unit 1	Unit 2	Unit 3		ALPHABETICAL ORDER
1.	BraceMarcus	Lon			BraceMarcus Lon
2.	BraceMason	Fred			BraceMason Fred
3.	Silas	MarkBrent			BradeMilkins Frederick
4.	Marcos	Lon	Brent		Marcos Lon Brent
5.	BradeMilkins	Frederick			Silas MarkBrent

✔ SELF-CHECK • Review Exercise 1

	Unit 1	Unit 2	Unit 3		ALPHABETICAL ORDER	RULE
1.	Breen	Sharon	Jean		Breen	1, 3
2.	Breene	S	T		Breen Sharon Jean	1, 3
3.	StRafter	Jason			Breene S	1, 3
4.	Breen				Breene S T	1, 3
5.	SansRafter	Joan			dAquisto Lonnie	1, 2, 4
6.	dAquisto	Lonnie			deRoyal Susie	1, 2, 4
7.	deRoyal	Susie			Rafter W Breene	1
8.	SanMichaels	Geo			SanMichaels Geo	1, 2, 4
9.	Breene	S			SansRafter Joan	1, 4, 5
10.	Rafter	W	Breene		StRafter Jason	1, 4

	Unit 1	Unit 2	Unit 3	ALPHABETICAL ORDER	RULE
1.	Braun	WilmaJean		Braun	1, 3
2.	elDorado	Maxine		Braun WilmaJean	1, 3, 5
3.	SteLorraine	Jonathon		Braune S	1, 3
4.	Braun			Brauning A B	1
5.	StLaurence	Chas		Brauning M	1
6.	Braune	S		Dawkins S Braune	1
7.	Brauning	M		elDorado Maxine	1, 4
8.	Dawkins	S	Braune	SansLaurence Michael	1, 5
9.	SansLaurence	Michael		SteLorraine Jonathon	1, 4
10.	Brauning	A	B	StLaurence Chas	1, 2, 4

 SELF-CHECK• Exercise 6

	Unit 1	Unit 2	Unit 3	ALPHABETICAL ORDER
1.	Right	Fairly		Frank Ramond
2.	Right	Olna	Faith	Ramondo Franco
3.	Riew	Mew	Leu	Riew Mew Leu
4.	Frank	Ramond		Right Fairly
5.	Ramondo	Franco		Right Olna Faith

 SELF-CHECK• Exercise 7

	Unit 1	Unit 2	Unit 3	Unit 4	ALPHABETICAL ORDER
1.	Jones	B	T	III	Jonas Brett T Jr
2.	Jones	B	T	4th	Jonas Brett T Sr
3.	Jonas	Brett	T	Jr	Jones B T 4th
4.	Jones	B	T	II	Jones B T II
5.	Jonas	Brett	T	Sr	Jones B T III

✔ SELF-CHECK • Exercise 8

	Unit 1	Unit 2	Unit 3	ALPHABETICAL ORDER
1.	Angelo	Martin	Mr	Angelo Judie Mrs
2.	Angelo	Judie	Mrs	Angelo Martin Dr
3.	Martin	Angelo	Major	Angelo Martin Mr
4.	Angelo	Martin	Dr	Martin Angelo Major
5.	Martin	Angelo	PhD	Martin Angelo PhD

✔ SELF-CHECK • Exercise 9

	Unit 1	Unit 2	ALPHABETICAL ORDER
1.	Queen	Victoria	Brother Victor
2.	Brothers	Victor	Brothers Victor
3.	Prof	Analytical	Prof Analytical
4.	Sister	Anna	Queen Victoria
5.	Brother	Victor	Sister Anna

✔ SELF-CHECK • Exercise 10

	Unit 1	Unit 2	Unit 3	Unit 4	Unit 5	Unit 6
1.	Jefferson	Lamar	Bradley	Indiana	Landmark Place	228
2.	Jefferson	Lamar	Bradley	Iowa	Landmark Street	2820
3.	Jefferson	Lamar	Bradley	Iowa	Landmark Street	1630
4.	Jefferson	Lamar	Bradley	Illinois	Long Circle	486
5.	Jefferson	Lamar	Bradley	Iowa	Zenith Street	1500

ALPHABETICAL ORDER

Jefferson Lamar Bradley Illinois 486 Long Circle

Jefferson Lamar Bradley Indiana 228 Landmark Place

Jefferson Lamar Bradley Iowa 1630 Landmark Street

Jefferson Lamar Bradley Iowa 2820 Landmark Street

Jefferson Lamar Bradley Iowa 1500 Zenith Street

✓ SELF-CHECK • Review Exercise 2

	Unit 1	Unit 2	Unit 3	Unit 4	Unit 5	Unit 6
1.	Biles	Lela	Columbus	Ohio	Zephyr Street	201
2.	Duchess	Beatrice				
3.	Billey	Ronald	Jr			
4.	Biles	Lela	Columbus	Ohio	Zephyr Street	221
5.	Biles	Leland	PhD			
6.	Billey	Ronald	3rd			
7.	Doctor	Fixit				
8.	Billey	Ronald	Sr			
9.	Biles	Leland	Dr			
10.	Bilaufa	Reyno				

ALPHABETICAL ORDER	RULE
Bilaufa Reyno	6
Biles Lela Columbus Ohio 201 Zephyr Street	10
Biles Lela Columbus Ohio 221 Zephyr Street	10
Biles Leland Dr	8
Biles Leland PhD	8
Billey Ronald 3rd	7
Billey Ronald Jr	7
Billey Ronald Sr	7
Doctor Fixit	9
Duchess Beatrice	9

✓ SELF-CHECK • Reinforcement Exercise 2

	Unit 1	Unit 2	Unit 3	Unit 4	Unit 5	Unit 6
1.	Kingsley	James	Orlando	Florida	Center Street	600
2.	King	James				
3.	King	Jadeth	Jr			
4.	Kingsley	James	Orlando	Florida	Peak Street	460
5.	James	Kingston	MD			
6.	King	Jadeth	3rd			
7.	Sheik	Jamal				
8.	King	Jadeth	Sr			
9.	James	Kingston	PhD			
10.	King	James	Mrs			

ALPHABETICAL ORDER	RULE
James Kingston MD	8
James Kingston PhD	8
King Jadeth 3rd	7
King Jadeth Jr	7
King Jadeth Sr	7
King James	9
King James Mrs	8
Kingsley James Orlando Florida 600 Center Street	10
Kingsley James Orlando Florida 460 Peak Street	10
Sheik Jamal	6

✔ SELF-CHECK • Exercise 11

Unit 1	Unit 2	Unit 3	Unit 4		ALPHABETICAL ORDER
1. Bean	Pot	Company			A Aggasi Sports Company
2. Ann	Byers	Music	Company		Amplifier Works The
3. Amplifier	Works	The			Andrews Machines Incorporated
4. A	Aggasi	Sports	Company		Ann Byers Music Company
5. Andrews	Machines	Incorporated			Bean Pot Company

✔ SELF-CHECK • Exercise 12

Unit 1	Unit 2	Unit 3	Unit 4		ALPHABETICAL ORDER
1. C	U	Glass	Inc		C O Cooking Company
2. C	O	Cooking	Company		C U Glass Inc
3. Chas	C	Class	Co		CCC Developers
4. Colde	Mfg	Co			Chas C Class Co
5. CCC	Developers				Colde Mfg Co

✔ SELF-CHECK • Exercise 13

Unit 1	Unit 2	Unit 3		ALPHABETICAL ORDER
1. BiggerBargains	Food	Shoppe		BigerFox Co
2. BigerFox	Co			BiggerBargains Food Shoppe
3. ByeNBuy	Baby	Store		BigoniaFox Publishing
4. BigTop	Circus			BigTop Circus
5. BigoniaFox	Publishing			ByeNBuy Baby Store

✔ SELF-CHECK • Exercise 14

	Unit 1	Unit 2	Unit 3	Unit 4
1.	Northern	Heat	Company	
2.	North	East	Gas	Co
3.	Southeast	Bean	Company	
4.	Southern	Hats	Inc	
5.	North	South	Systems	

ALPHABETICAL ORDER
North East Gas Co
North South Systems
Northern Heat Company
Southeast Bean Company
Southern Hats Inc

✔ SELF-CHECK • Exercise 15

	Unit 1	Unit 2	Unit 3
1.	DesPlaines	Publishing	Co
2.	TerreHaute	Book	Store
3.	SantaFe	Cattle	Company
4.	ElPaso	Bus	Lines
5.	SanBernadoni	Fruit	Growers

ALPHABETICAL ORDER
DesPlaines Publishing Co
ElPaso Bus Lines
SanBernadoni Fruit Growers
SantaFe Cattle Company
TerreHaute Book Store

✔ SELF-CHECK • Review Exercise 3

	Unit 1	Unit 2	Unit 3	Unit 4
1.	SanDiego	Sand	Co	
2.	Southeast	Junque	Store	
3.	LaneStarr	Belt	Co	
4.	LAFF	Gag	Store	
5.	See	U	Later	Cafe
6.	South	West	Beverages	
7.	L	L	Gaff	Brokers
8.	SeeULater	Optical	Co	
9.	LasVegas	Candy	Shop	
10.	Lolly	Gag	Cafe	The

ALPHABETICAL ORDER	RULE
L L Gaff Brokers	11, 12
LAFF Gag Store	11
LaneStarr Belt Co	12, 13
LasVegas Candy Shop	15
Lolly Gag Cafe The	11
SanDiego Sand Co	12, 15
See U Later Cafe	12
SeeULater Optical Co	13
South West Beverages	14
Southeast Junque Store	14

✔ SELF-CHECK • Reinforcement Exercise 3

	Unit 1	Unit 2	Unit 3	Unit 4	ALPHABETICAL ORDER	RULE
1.	L	Briley	Music	Co	East West Knit Shop	14
2.	LookUsOver	Decorators			EasternDay Hobby Shoppe	13
3.	ElDorado	Tea	Co		Elden Crest Food Store	11
4.	EasternDay	Hobby	Shoppe		ElDorado Tea Co	12, 15
5.	Lotta	House	Cafe	The	L Briley Music Co	11, 12
6.	Elden	Crest	Food	Store	L O T Binders	12
7.	L	O	T	Binders	Local Motion Inc	11, 12
8.	East	West	Knit	Shop	LookUsOver Decorators	13
9.	Lotus	Blossom	Cosmetics		Lotta House Cafe The	11
10.	Local	Motion	Inc		Lotus Blossom Cosmetics	11

✔ SELF-CHECK • Exercise 16

	Unit 1	Unit 2	Unit 3	Unit 4	ALPHABETICAL ORDER
1.	Cost	Plus	Distributors		Cost Plus Distributors
2.	Dollar	Rental	Co		Costner and Caffrey Realtors
3.	Costner	and	Caffrey	Realtors	Cozy Number Cafe
4.	Cozy	Number	Cafe		Dollar Rental Co
5.	Doller	and	Ryan	Attorneys	Doller and Ryan Attorneys

✔ SELF-CHECK • Exercise 17

	Unit 1	Unit 2	Unit 3	Unit 4	ALPHABETICAL ORDER
1.	Desis	Deli			DecOTrim Cabinetry
2.	DiscoDance	Fever	Inc		Desis Deli
3.	Dishes	Drapes	Drains	Ltd	DiscoDance Fever Inc
4.	Dont	Panic	Movers		Dishes Drapes Drains Ltd
5.	DecOTrim	Cabinetry			Dont Panic Movers

✔ SELF-CHECK • Exercise 18

	Unit 1	Unit 2	Unit 3	Unit 4	Unit 5	Unit 6
1.	Cozy	Cafe	Ames	Iowa	Leland Avenue	2740
2.	Cellular	Ltd	Rockford	Illinois	Falcon Road	6800
3.	Cozy	Cafe	Ames	Alabama	Leland Avenue	2740
4.	Cellular	Ltd	Rockford	Illinois	Falcon Road	117
5.	Cozy	Cafe	Ames	Alabama	Leland Avenue	212

ALPHABETICAL ORDER

Cellular Ltd Rockford Illinois 117 Falcon Road

Cellular Ltd Rockford Illinois 6800 Falcon Road

Cozy Cafe Ames Alabama 212 Leland Avenue

Cozy Cafe Ames Alabama 2740 Leland Avenue

Cozy Cafe Ames Iowa 2740 Leland Avenue

✔ SELF-CHECK • Exercise 19

	Unit 1	Unit 2	Unit 3	Unit 4		ALPHABETICAL ORDER
1.	Two	Tunes	Music	Co		1 Supermarket
2.	Texas	Tailors	Inc			12 Trees Trailer Park
3.	Twelve	Days	Cafe			Texas Tailors Inc
4.	1	Supermarket				Twelve Days Cafe
5.	12	Trees	Trailer	Park		Two Tunes Music Co

✔ SELF-CHECK • Exercise 20

	Unit 1	Unit 2	Unit 3	Unit 4	Unit 5
1.	Maine	State	of	Civil	Division
2.	United	States	Government	Naval	Department
3.	Monroe	Police	Department		
4.	Montrose	County	Water	Department	
5.	United	States	Government	Veterans	Administration

ALPHABETICAL ORDER

Maine State of Civil Division

Monroe Police Department

Montrose County Water Department

United States Government Naval Department

United States Government Veterans Administration

	Unit 1	Unit 2	Unit 3	Unit 4	Unit 5	Unit 6
1.	Utah	Environmental	Department			
2.	Uriahs	Digging	Service			
3.	Threatt	Textiles	Lawson	Utah	Hunt Street	68
4.	Underwood	and	Blake	Co		
5.	United	States	Government	Postal	Service	
6.	Ten	Ton	Trucks	Inc		
7.	Threatt	Textiles	Lawson	Utah	Hobson Street	740
8.	10	Street	Fine	Foods		
9.	Union	City	Sanitation	Department		
10.	Three	Dollar	Ties	Inc		

ALPHABETICAL ORDER	RULE
10 Street Fine Foods	19
Ten Ton Trucks Inc	19
Threatt Textiles Lawson Utah 740 Hobson Street	18
Threatt Textiles Lawson Utah 68 Hunt Street	18
Three Dollar Ties Inc	12, 16, 19
Underwood and Blake Co	16
Union City Sanitation Department	20
United States Government Postal Service	20
Uriahs Digging Service	17
Utah Environmental Department	20

✔ SELF-CHECK • Reinforcement Exercise 4

	Unit 1	Unit 2	Unit 3	Unit 4	Unit 5	Unit 6
1.	United	States	Government	Defense	Department	
2.	Mississippi	State	of	Health	Department	
3.	Mells	Delicatessen				
4.	Dollar	Meal	Deli			
5.	Meltons	Brick	Company			
6.	Uglys	Stained	Furniture			
7.	Mannys	Subs	Millville	Ohio	Rose Street	16
8.	Sixteen	Candles	Music	Shop		
9.	Mannys	Subs	Millville	Maine	Rose Street	16
10.	16	Motel				

ALPHABETICAL ORDER	RULE
16 Motel	19
Dollar Meal Deli	16
Mannys Subs Millville Maine 16 Rose Street	17, 18
Mannys Subs Millville Ohio 16 Rose Street	17, 18
Mells Delicatessen	17
Meltons Brick Company	17
Mississippi State of Health Department	20
Sixteen Candles Music Shop	19
Uglys Stained Furniture	17
United States Government Defense Department	20

✔ SELF-CHECK • Exercise 21

Letter(s) not yet released: 2, 6

Letter No.	Unit 1	Unit 2	Unit 3
1	Accurate	Publishers	Inc
2	Eversolls	Bakery	
3	Drexel	Company	The
4	Crockery	Shoppe	The
5	CUE	Promotional	Products
6	Brakley	Music	Distributors
7	Electic	Agency	
8	AZ	Market	Research
9	Alliance	Promotions	Inc
10	Accurate	Publishers	Inc

✔ SELF-CHECK • Exercise 22

Letter numbers as they appear in the folders, front to back:

1. Accurate Publishers Inc: 10, 1
2. A–B folder: 9, 8, 6
3. CUE Promotional Products: 5
4. C–D folder: 4, 3
5. Electic Agency: 7
6. E–F folder: 2

✔ SELF-CHECK • Exercise 23

Letter(s) not yet released: 17
Letter numbers as they appear in the folders, front to back:

1. Accurate Publishers Inc: 10, 1
2. A–B folder: 18, 9, 17, 20, 8, 14, 6
3. CUE Promotional Products: 5
4. C–D folder: 4, 15, 13, 19, 3
5. Electic Agency: 7
6. E–F folder: 11, 16, 2, 14X, 12

✔ SELF-CHECK • Exercise 24

	Letter Number	Folder Caption	Filed Behind Letter	Filed in Front of Letter
1.	20	A–B	17	8
2.	15	C–D	4	13
3.	2	E–F	16	14X
4.	14	A–B	8	6
5.	13	C–D	15	19

✔ SELF-CHECK • Exercise 25

Letter(s) not yet released: 23
Letter numbers as they appear in the folders, front to back:

1. Accurate Publishers Inc.:   28, 10, 1
2. A–B folder: 27, 26, 23, 18, 9, 21, 17, 20, 8, 14, 26X, 6
3. CUE Promotional Products: 24, 5
4. C–D folder: 22, 4, 15, 25, 13, 19, 3
5. Electic Agency: 29, 7
6. E–F folder: 30, 11, 16, 2, 14X, 12

☑ SELF-CHECK • Exercise 26

	Letter Number	Folder Caption	Filed Behind Letter	Filed in Front of Letter
1.	10	Accurate Publishers Inc	28	1
2.	9	A–B	18	21
3.	5	CUE Promotional Products	24	22 (first letter in C–D folder)
4.	16	E–F	11	2
5.	3	C–D	19	29

☑ SELF-CHECK • Exercise 27

1. Letter 51:   C:\LETTERS\MICHIGAN\PONTIAC
2. Letter 54:   C:\LETTERS\MISSOURI\STLOUIS
3. Letter 56:   C:\LETTERS\MICHIGAN\FLINT
4. Letter 57:   C:\LETTERS\MINNESOTA\DULUTH
5. Letter 58:   C:\LETTERS\MONTANA\BILLINGS
6. Letter 59:   C:\LETTERS\MINNESOTA\MINNEAPOLIS
7. Letter 61:   C:\LETTERS\MICHIGAN\PALMS
8. Letter 62:   C:\LETTERS\MONTANA\BUTTE
9. Letter 65:   C:\LETTERS\MISSOURI\WINSLOW

Answers to Fast-Find Exercises

FAST-FIND • Exercise 1

1. 3
2. 7
3. 1
4. 2
5. 20
6. 18
7. 15
8. 19
9. 5
10. 9

FAST-FIND • Exercise 2

1. 29
2. 27
3. 11
4. 40
5. 38
6. 21
7. 31
8. 33
9. 23
10. 17

FAST-FIND • Exercise 3

1. 44
2. 45
3. 10
4. 37
5. 22
6. 32
7. 14
8. 54
9. 36
10. 53

FAST-FIND • Exercise 4

1. 49
2. 93
3. 78
4. 64
5. 13
6. 80
7. 42
8. 40
9. 77
10. 91

FAST-FIND • Exercise 5

1. 39
2. 21
3. 9
4. 24
5. 47
6. 14
7. 4
8. 8
9. 30
10. 26

FAST-FIND • Exercise 6

1. 84
2. 91
3. 86
4. 88
5. 83
6. 82
7. 89

Name _____ Date _____

Write your name and the current date in the blanks above. Index and alphabetize the following names in the proper blanks. This checkup is based on filing rules 1–5.

	Names	Unit 1	Unit 2	Unit 3	ALPHABETICAL ORDER
1.	Paula G. MacNelson				
2.	Chas. J. Severnson				
3.	Joanne Gant-Carter				
4.	A. M. Lincolnson				
5.	Jerry Malcombe				
6.	Eliot San John				
7.	Sean L. Merrick				
8.	Barbara Jean Gant				
9.	Benj. Samuel Lidenl				
10.	J. V. O'Donald				
11.	Dora B. Saxe				
12.	Albert McGivens				
13.	D. B. Saxen				
14.	Ann-Marie Lincolnson				
15.	Barbette Judith Gant				
16.	Anne O'Donald				
17.	James St. Cinto				
18.	Allen John Olson				
19.	A. Marie Lincolnson				
20.	Annie Severns				

Name _____ Date _____

Write your name and the current date in the blanks above. Index and alphabetize the following names in the proper blanks. This checkup is based on filing rules 1–10.

Names	Unit 1	Unit 2	Unit 3	Unit 4	Unit 5	Unit 6
1. Helen Dodds 613 Adams Road Akron, Ohio						
2. Wm. R. Fajey						
3. Robert A. Kim						
4. Dr. Times-up						
5. Jane Thomas						
6. Father Tom						
7. H. Mark Dodds						
8. Raja Fakhr						
9. King Philip						
10. Robt. Kim						
11. Judge Wm. R. Fajey						
12. Helen Dodds 74 Adams Road Akron, Vermont						
13. Shui Chi Tome						
14. Wm. R. Fajey, Sr.						
15. Professor Jane Thomas						
16. Phillip King						
17. Helen Dodds 1469 Adams Road Akron, Ohio						
18. Louise King-Davis						
19. Wm. R. Fajey, II						
20. Dong Won Kim						

_____

_____

_____

_____

_____

_____

_____

_____

_____

_____

_____

_____

_____

_____

_____

_____

_____

Name _____ Date _____

Write your name and the current date in the blanks above. Index and alphabetize the following names in the proper blanks. This checkup is based on filing rules 1–15.

	Names	Unit 1	Unit 2	Unit 3	Unit 4	Unit 5	Unit 6
1.	Santa Fe Gear						
2.	The Tabletop Inn						
3.	On-Line Data Systems						
4.	S and L Co.						
5.	South East Sailors, Inc.						
6.	Skin-Care, Inc.						
7.	Maria-Luise Santana						
8.	Jean O'Neill 916 Bayshore Road Dallas, Texas						
9.	Touch of Glass Antiques						
10.	Thos. Sabel Mgmt. Co.						
11.	Southeast Container Co.						
12.	SJC Printing Company						
13.	Sister Rose						
14.	San Pedro Roofing, Inc.						
15.	On Time Travel						
16.	T-L-C Tours						
17.	The Overbrook Restaurant						
18.	Nassa Sheriff						
19.	South Shore Investment Corp.						
20.	Jean O'Neill 1145 Bayshore Road Dallas, Texas						

Proficiency Checkup 4

Name _____ Date _____

Write your name and the current date in the blanks above. Index and alphabetized the following names in the proper blanks. This checkup is based on filing rules 1–20.

Names	Unit 1	Unit 2	Unit 3	Unit 4	Unit 5	Unit 6
1. Four-Five Motel	_____	_____	_____	_____	_____	_____
2. St. Louis Blues Deli	_____	_____	_____	_____	_____	_____
3. Utah Department of Research	_____	_____	_____	_____	_____	_____
4. 4th Avenue Food Store	_____	_____	_____	_____	_____	_____
5. Blake's Bulletins 1000 El Cerito Austin, Texas	_____	_____	_____	_____	_____	_____
6. Casey's Casuals, Inc.	_____	_____	_____	_____	_____	_____
7. 12th Hour Caterers, Inc.	_____	_____	_____	_____	_____	_____
8. San Jose Health Department	_____	_____	_____	_____	_____	_____
9. Cynthia L. Unger-Ziff	_____	_____	_____	_____	_____	_____
10. Charles S. Bloke	_____	_____	_____	_____	_____	_____
11. Four Freedoms Book Store	_____	_____	_____	_____	_____	_____
12. Blake's Bulletins 1163 El Cerito Brownsville, Texas	_____	_____	_____	_____	_____	_____
13. Dr. Charles S. Bloke	_____	_____	_____	_____	_____	_____
14. USA Furniture	_____	_____	_____	_____	_____	_____
15. Chas. Bloke & Sons, Inc.	_____	_____	_____	_____	_____	_____
16. 20-20 Eye Specialists, Inc.	_____	_____	_____	_____	_____	_____
17. Unger & Ziff Drug Store	_____	_____	_____	_____	_____	_____
18. ¢ Off Curtains	_____	_____	_____	_____	_____	_____
19. C B Software Co.	_____	_____	_____	_____	_____	_____
20. Four-Fifteen Motel	_____	_____	_____	_____	_____	_____

_____

_____

_____

_____

_____

_____

_____

_____

_____

_____

_____

_____

_____

_____

_____

_____

_____

_____

_____

Name _____ Date _____

PRACTICAL APPLICATION 1 • Answer Sheet

List the numbers of the cards in the order in which you have arranged them, front to back.

1. _____   6. _____   11. _____   16. _____

2. _____   7. _____   12. _____   17. _____

3. _____   8. _____   13. _____   18. _____

4. _____   9. _____   14. _____   19. _____

5. _____   10. _____   15. _____   20. _____

Name _____ Date _____

PRACTICAL APPLICATION 2 • Answer Sheet

List the numbers of the cards in the order in which you have arranged them, front to back.

1. _____   6. _____   11. _____   16. _____

2. _____   7. _____   12. _____   17. _____

3. _____   8. _____   13. _____   18. _____

4. _____   9. _____   14. _____   19. _____

5. _____   10. _____   15. _____   20. _____

PRACTICAL APPLICATION 3 • Answer Sheet

List the numbers of the cards in the order in which you have arranged them, front to back.

1. _____	11. _____	21. _____	31. _____
2. _____	12. _____	22. _____	32. _____
3. _____	13. _____	23. _____	33. _____
4. _____	14. _____	24. _____	34. _____
5. _____	15. _____	25. _____	35. _____
6. _____	16. _____	26. _____	36. _____
7. _____	17. _____	27. _____	37. _____
8. _____	18. _____	28. _____	38. _____
9. _____	19. _____	29. _____	39. _____
10. _____	20. _____	30. _____	40. _____

Name _____ Date _____

PRACTICAL APPLICATION 4 • Answer Sheet

List the numbers of the cards in the order in which you have arranged them, front to back.

1. _____	6. _____	11. _____	16. _____
2. _____	7. _____	12. _____	17. _____
3. _____	8. _____	13. _____	18. _____
4. _____	9. _____	14. _____	19. _____
5. _____	10. _____	15. _____	20. _____

Name _____ Date _____

PRACTICAL APPLICATION 5 • Answer Sheet

List the numbers of the cards in the order in which you have arranged them, front to back.

1. _____	11. _____	21. _____	31. _____	41. _____	51. _____
2. _____	12. _____	22. _____	32. _____	42. _____	52. _____
3. _____	13. _____	23. _____	33. _____	43. _____	53. _____
4. _____	14. _____	24. _____	34. _____	44. _____	54. _____
5. _____	15. _____	25. _____	35. _____	45. _____	55. _____
6. _____	16. _____	26. _____	36. _____	46. _____	56. _____
7. _____	17. _____	27. _____	37. _____	47. _____	57. _____
8. _____	18. _____	28. _____	38. _____	48. _____	58. _____
9. _____	19. _____	29. _____	39. _____	49. _____	59. _____
10. _____	20. _____	30. _____	40. _____	50. _____	60. _____

Name _____ Date _____

PRACTICAL APPLICATION 6 • Answer Sheet

List the numbers of the cards in the order in which you have arranged them, front to back.

1. _____	10. _____	19. _____	28. _____
2. _____	11. _____	20. _____	29. _____
3. _____	12. _____	21. _____	30. _____
4. _____	13. _____	22. _____	31. _____
5. _____	14. _____	23. _____	32. _____
6. _____	15. _____	24. _____	33. _____
7. _____	16. _____	25. _____	34. _____
8. _____	17. _____	26. _____	35. _____
9. _____	18. _____	27. _____	36. _____

Name _____   Date _____

PRACTICAL APPLICATION 7 • Answer Sheet

List the numbers of the cards in the order in which you arranged them, front to back.

Card No.	Card No.	Card No.	Card No.	Card No.	Card No.
1. _____	11. _____	21. _____	31. _____	41. _____	51. _____
2. _____	12. _____	22. _____	32. _____	42. _____	52. _____
3. _____	13. _____	23. _____	33. _____	43. _____	53. _____
4. _____	14. _____	24. _____	34. _____	44. _____	54. _____
5. _____	15. _____	25. _____	35. _____	45. _____	55. _____
6. _____	16. _____	26. _____	36. _____	46. _____	56. _____
7. _____	17. _____	27. _____	37. _____	47. _____	57. _____
8. _____	18. _____	28. _____	38. _____	48. _____	58. _____
9. _____	19. _____	29. _____	39. _____	49. _____	59. _____
10. _____	20. _____	30. _____	40. _____	50. _____	60. _____

(Continued)

Name _____   Date _____

OPTIONAL PRACTICAL APPLICATION • Answer Sheet

List the numbers of the cards in the order in which you arranged them, front to back.

Card No.	Card No.	Card No.	Card No.
1. _____	11. _____	21. _____	31. _____
2. _____	12. _____	22. _____	32. _____
3. _____	13. _____	23. _____	33. _____
4. _____	14. _____	24. _____	34. _____
5. _____	15. _____	25. _____	35. _____
6. _____	16. _____	26. _____	36. _____
7. _____	17. _____	27. _____	37. _____
8. _____	18. _____	28. _____	38. _____
9. _____	19. _____	29. _____	39. _____
10. _____	20. _____	30. _____	40. _____

Card No.	Card No.	Card No.	Card No.	Card No.	Card No.
61. _____	67. _____	73. _____	79. _____	85. _____	91. _____
62. _____	68. _____	74. _____	80. _____	86. _____	92. _____
63. _____	69. _____	75. _____	81. _____	87. _____	93. _____
64. _____	70. _____	76. _____	82. _____	88. _____	94. _____
65. _____	71. _____	77. _____	83. _____	89. _____	95. _____
66. _____	72. _____	78. _____	84. _____	90. _____	96. _____

Name _____ Date _____

PRACTICAL APPLICATION 8 • Answer Sheet

Letter(s) not yet released: _____

Letter numbers as they appear in the folders, front to back:

1. Accurate Publishers, Inc.:   _____

2. A–B folder: _____

3. CUE Promotional Products: _____

4. C–D folder: _____

5. Electic Agency: _____

6. E–F folder: _____

Name _____ Date _____

PRACTICAL APPLICATION 9 • Answer Sheet

Letter(s) not yet released: _____

List in order from front to back the letters that would be placed behind the following state guides:

1. Michigan: _____

2. Minnesota: _____

3. Missouri: _____

4. Montana: _____

Name _____ Date _____

PRACTICAL APPLICATION 10 • Answer Sheet

Letter(s) not yet released: _____

List in order from front to back the letters that would be placed behind the following primary subject headings:

1. Books: _____

2. Cafes: _____

3. Music: _____

Name _____ Date _____

PRACTICAL APPLICATION 11 • Answer Sheet

List the numbers of the cards in the order in which you have arranged them, front to back:

1. Company Policies: _____

2. Customer Relations: _____

3. Supervision: _____

4. Telephone Usage: _____

Filing Checklist

Remember to perform these steps before filing any document.

1. *Examine the letter.* Is this an incoming or outgoing letter? If it is an incoming letter, does it have a release mark? If not, return it to the person responsible for handling the letter.
2. *Index the letter.* Determine the filing units under which it will be filed.
   a. For outgoing letters, choose the filing units from the inside address.
   b. For incoming letters, choose the filing units from the letterhead.
3. *Code the letter.*
4. *Check the letter to see if it needs to be cross-referenced.* If so, prepare a cross-reference sheet.
5. *Remove any paper clips or rubber bands.* If necessary, staple any multi-page documents together.
6. *Sort the correspondence according to the filing system being used.*
7. *File the correspondence.*
   a. Did you place the correspondence in the correct individual or miscellaneous folder?
   b. Did you arrange the correspondence so that the most recent date is in front of the folder?
   c. Did you place the letterhead or top of the document on the left side of the folder?
8. *Check file folder capacity regularly.* If a miscellaneous folder becomes too thick, create individual folders for frequent correspondents.

STATE ABBREVIATIONS

State	Two-Letter Abbreviation	State	Two-Letter Abbreviation
Alabama	AL	Montana	MT
Alaska	AK	Nebraska	NE
Arizona	AZ	Nevada	NV
Arkansas	AR	New Hampshire	NH
California	CA	New Jersey	NJ
Colorado	CO	New Mexico	NM
Connecticut	CT	New York	NY
Delaware	DE	North Carolina	NC
Florida	FL	North Dakota	ND
Georgia	GA	Ohio	OH
Hawaii	HI	Oklahoma	OK
Idaho	ID	Oregon	OR
Illinois	IL	Pennsylvania	PA
Indiana	IN	Rhode Island	RI
Iowa	IA	South Carolina	SC
Kansas	KS	South Dakota	SD
Kentucky	KY	Tennessee	TN
Louisiana	LA	Texas	TX
Maine	ME	Utah	UT
Maryland	MD	Vermont	VT
Massachusetts	MA	Virginia	VA
Michigan	MI	Washington	WA
Minnesota	MN	West Virginia	WV
Mississippi	MS	Wisconsin	WI
Missouri	MO	Wyoming	WY